BACK
TO
CHURCH

BACK
TO
CHURCH

A CALL TO THOSE WHO HAVE LEFT
AND
THOSE WHO HAVE STAYED

CARA LUECHT

WhiteFire
PUBLISHING

TABLE OF CONTENTS

CHAPTER ONE

A STARTING POINT

I grew up in a Christian household. Not just any Christian household. I grew up in one of those families that didn't go to dances, whose parents never drank, and who sat down to family dinners every night. When I was a kid, I didn't join sports or do any school activities that had Wednesday evening or Sunday obligations. I had two parents who loved me and my siblings. I was protected against many of the harsher realities of life. Of my peer group, I can say I was one of the few who experienced childhood without the trauma of divorce, addiction issues, tragic parenting techniques, or some kind of abuse.

My father was a Pentecostal preacher who typically drew crowds of just under a hundred people. My mother was a stay-at-home pastor's wife who did an admirable job at the religious version of keeping-up-with-the-Joneses—which was a feat for the wife of a preacher of modest means in the era of Tammy Faye Bakker. Being a pastor's wife in the

80s could be demanding, and my mother excelled in many ways. Although she didn't play piano (a standard for the 1980s pastor's wife), she did sing, and she made sure that her daughters took piano lessons. And even though she dealt with her own insecurities, she taught women's groups and Sunday school classes and played an endless number of support roles for my dad.

My dad was old school but struggled commendably with the legalism that tended to be his default position. Like us, he grew up in the Church, but he grew up in an era when his first trip to the movies in 1963 to see *Son of Flubber* meant that he spent the entire time in the back row, by himself, praying that Jesus didn't come back until the movie was over and he had a chance to pray for forgiveness.

For us, the outcome of this culture of legalism played out in things like his begrudging approvals when we asked to go roller-skating because he knew that there would be secular music, and he didn't want us listening to it. But more than that, he didn't want us growing up to think we'd go to hell if we did listen to it.

In short, my parents did a good job. And if you are coming to this book because you are expecting another Pentecostal kid to write about their escape from the tyranny of the Church, you're going to be disappointed.

I still love Jesus. Church camp was awesome. And now I am a Pentecostal preacher myself.

It was not an easy journey, though, and my faith looks

a lot different now than it did at the beginning, but I suppose that's the point.

QUESTIONS I COULDN'T ANSWER

I never wanted to go into ministry. More than that, I *actively* didn't want to go into ministry.

I grew up as a preacher's kid—or PK for short—and I knew that it wasn't the kind of life that anyone in their right mind would pursue. It's hard. There is no money in it (unless you are a televangelist or mega-church pastor). People can be jerks. And in the Church, those jerks can be even more difficult to deal with because they're fueled by righteous indignation. So, justified jerks. Fun.

Then my dad decided he was ready to retire.

I had served in the church as a worship leader for nearly two decades, so I knew, following standard practices during a leadership transition, when my dad left, my husband and I would also need to find a different place.

After considering our options, we visited a few local churches and listened to online sermons. What I found surprised me.

There are some exceptionally good churches out there, and the last few years have given me the opportunity to get to know many pastors and congregations who are diligent in their mission to spread the gospel. But six years ago, they evaded me.

When I began searching for a new church, I listened to

sermons that blamed disease on a lack of faith. Sermons that blatantly misused Scripture. Pastors who gave altar calls for salvation and never mentioned repentance. Churches that no longer celebrated communion as a community. Worship bands that led songs with pretty words but horrible theology. And prayers for salvation that sounded like joining a country club where all the members enjoyed an abundant, successful life as defined by human standards.

Part of my challenge in finding a new church family was that I had basically been in the same church for most of my life. Looking back, I think I was somewhat of a snob about it all. I was frustrated by the things I knew were wrong, and I allowed my frustrations to color my opinion of the churches I visited. But one thing I have learned is that God uses our good and our bad, and this time he was using my overly critical mindset to stir something that I had not considered for a long time.

With a love of learning that stretches back as far as I can remember, I have always returned to education when something doesn't make sense. And none of this journey that I had embarked on since my dad announced his retirement had made any sense at all. Church had changed. People had changed. But I knew that God had not changed. It was natural for me to start looking for a way to learn more about my beliefs and God in general.

I applied to seminary. It was easy to tell by the look on my parents' faces that they thought seminary was overkill, but I didn't care. At one point, my dad asked why I didn't simply take some Bible college courses online. It was here when I understood the problem and the first of what would be many questions solidified.

I didn't care about what I should believe. I had learned what to believe my whole life, and it had gotten me precisely to where I was standing at that point: no church, no community, and a faith that I could defend to the rafters, thanks to decades of training that resulted from the Church's obsession with apologetics, but no sense of why I believed any of it.

I knew the "what." I needed to know the "why."

Why did I believe what I had been taught? Why is Christianity different from other religions? Why do we worship at the altar? Why do we take communion? Why do we baptize? Why do we pray for others? Why do we say things like "faith the size of a mustard seed" and "lukewarm" and all the phrases that make no sense unless someone is part of the Church? And I didn't want the same pat answers that I'd heard over and over from other Christians who were offended that I even asked the questions.

I didn't need to listen to an apologist try to prove the existence of God. I had been listening to them for decades and watched all that information become useless in the lives of my friends and the students I taught when they faced hardships. I had been around long enough to know that argument does not have "keeping" power. The Holy Spirit does.

> ARGUMENT DOES NOT HAVE
> "KEEPING" POWER.
> THE HOLY SPIRIT DOES.

So how could we, as people who profess to walk with the Holy Spirit, miss the mark on so many levels?

We have the greatest story, the only one with a loving God who can make sense of all the problems in this world. So why was it that my college students (those from Christian homes) often asked if they could write their freshman English papers about science versus religion? Why were the homeschooled kids—the ones I thought would be the most solid in their beliefs—simply angry with the world? Why had the world become a burden for the people in the Church, instead of the gift that God had intended?

Why was everyone so threatened? If the battle has already been won...why did everyone act like the fate of their church rested on who was voted into a political office? Why were the people who had been sitting in the pews the longest also the most angry and impatient?

I was accepted into seminary, and I started studying.

One of my first classes asked every student what had pulled them into this kind of study.

I had to think a lot about that. My first "why" had led me to an expanding circle of other questions, but I synthesized it down to one that encompassed all the other issues: What makes a mature Christian?

CHAPTER TWO

THE MYTH OF MATURITY

I graduated from seminary at the end of 2018. Little did I know how many times over the next years I would return to that question of maturity.

Like most kids who grew up in the Church, I assumed that if you were old and if you had been a Christian for a long time, you were mature in your walk with Christ. After all, "old" and "mature" seem to go together naturally.

When I began looking for other churches (before I had started seminary), and I realized that we—as the Church—have difficulty answering the most basic "why" questions about our faith, I suspected that we were not as mature as we thought.

And 2020 cemented my suspicions.

The year the pandemic began, I watched people (old and young) in the Church who had been friends for decades torn apart over social media posts. Politics, health emergencies (or lack thereof, depending on your politics), isolation, racial tensions, and simple things like masks made people who had been Christians their entire life completely unrecognizable as such. I read scorn-filled posts from people who had, three months prior, been teaching Bible studies. People stopped connecting with their church family because they disagreed about a cloth mask: if you wore a mask, you were faithless; if you didn't, you didn't care about others. Preachers traded in the gospel for politics. I prayed for pastors as they tried to navigate between people who called them racist because they wouldn't connect to a particular phrase, and I prayed for those who left the Church because their pastor happened to connect in a way they didn't agree with.

In short, the Church risked becoming unrecognizable as such because the gospel took a backseat to whatever the hot topic of the day happened to be. Looking back, we realize that this isn't new—but the isolation and restrictions of 2020 made what had been simmering and swelling underneath the surface bubble to the top at an alarming rate.

Sure, there were pockets of beauty—that's because God will reign in all things. Conversations about race opened that might have never happened. Friendships that were allowed to heal became stronger. And many of our assumptions were called into question, forcing us to reconsider some of our own practices and habits. But I don't think any of us would say, collectively, that we made it through those years having better demonstrated God's love to the world.

No matter how we define Christian maturity, there is a truth we cannot escape: Our maturity will be evidenced by our actions. James 2:26 makes this clear: "For just as the body without the spirit is dead, so faith without works is also dead" (NRSV). And when, as Christians, we parse out our recent past, we could have treated both those outside the Church and inside the Church better.

During times of little to no crisis, it was easy to consider ourselves good Christians. Most of us would have simply pointed to our behavior as proof. The problem is, pious living does not mean mature Christianity. Just because you can make it through your day without cursing in the grocery store doesn't mean that when you are facing a stressful situation at the checkout counter you will treat the cashier with the kind of love and consideration that points them to Christ.

Personal discipline does not necessarily mean that you are close to God. It means that you are compliant. That's not bad. And it goes along with maturity, but maturity in Christ can't happen without relationship, and if we are in relationship with Jesus, it's inescapable that our interactions with others will demonstrate it (John 13:35).

So, as I sat in my office at home, watching Facebook demonstrate everyone's worst to the world, I prayed for discernment and insight and any way not only to understand what was going on, but also to help those who were evidently not doing well.

I spoke with other pastors who recognized the same challenges within their congregations, and we realized that we are not innocent in all of this.

We had fallen into the same trap that our people had. We had assumed that because parishioners had been sitting under our teaching and attending our churches for decades that they were mature. The facts spoke otherwise, and maybe this calls our collective pride into a place of accountability. Where we expected to see compassion, we often saw the reverse. Where we expected to see patience, we often witnessed intolerance. And truthfully, we were disappointed in ourselves, in our people, and in the Church in general.

Even if your own church didn't experience these challenges, we can't ignore the data. The latest Barna survey revealed that 52 percent of churchgoers are looking forward to attending in-person services again.[11] That leaves 48 percent of the Church less-than-enthusiastic about coming back. Those are our brothers and sisters in Christ. Those are the ones who are saved, who understand the message of the cross, and who have spent their time and efforts within the body of believers.

If we can't even keep our own, then something has gone wrong. At the very least, this means that 48 percent of the people sitting in the pews do not have the basic understanding of the importance of the Christian community. If we are honest, though, it might be even bleaker. What if

---

[1] https://reachrightstudios.com/25-church-statistics-for-2021/#h-13-church-attendance-still-reeling-from-covid

the 48 percent who do not want to come back feel that way because of the actions or inactions of the other 52 percent?

If the number of articles written by those who have chosen not to come back to the Church is any indication, this is largely the case for a good number of Christians.

This speaks directly to maturity because community is at the very heart of understanding the gospel. Jesus never intended us to be perfectly behaved believers in isolation. Anyone can behave when all temptation and potential for conflict has been removed. We are supposed to be together and make each other better by building relationships. Iron sharpens iron (Proverbs 27:17). God made humanity in God's image and created us to have relationship with both God and other humans. Living in community is valuable *because* of the challenges.

A lack of conflict does not mean a congregation is mature. It could mean that everyone simply tolerates each other and no longer learns from each other. Or, maybe even more frightening, it could mean that there is an entire congregation who has grown to think the same things, to agree on the same opinions, maybe even to follow the same political leaders.

To mistake harmony for maturity is dangerous; God uses conflict to make us better suited for Kingdom work. If you are part of a congregation because that community thinks and feels exactly as you do, then you need to take a serious look at your own potential for growth. Likewise, if you have left a healthy congregation because they do not think and feel as you do, have you simply told God "No"?

Please do not misunderstand. Paul makes it clear that we are to live in unity. But unity is not achieved by robotic like-mindedness. Unity in the Church is achieved only when we celebrate our differences, learn from them, use them, and then put them aside when the time comes to serve others.

> UNITY IN THE CHURCH IS ACHIEVED ONLY WHEN WE CELEBRATE OUR DIFFERENCES, LEARN FROM THEM, USE THEM, AND THEN PUT THEM ASIDE WHEN THE TIME COMES TO SERVE OTHERS.

This leaves us with the question of how we have swallowed the myth of our own maturity so completely. And have done it for so long.

The rich young ruler's encounter with Christ in Luke 18:18-30 offers insight.

The scene begins with the rich man asking Jesus what he must do to inherit eternal life. Like any of us living relatively comfortably in a success-driven society, this young man probably had checked several things off his list. He was wealthy, successful by the standards of his peers, and he still had his youth. The next thing to conquer was securing eternal life.

It sounds arrogant to our ears, but if we are honest, how many times do we go to God with our own lists? God, I have grown beyond my addictions, I have volunteered my time, I am a good person. What can I do next? What thing do you want from me?

But Jesus was not fooled by the rich young ruler's pride-laced question. God wants all of us, even our strivings. Especially our strivings. There is no list. There is nothing to check off. The first commandment is to have no other gods before us. This includes the gods of our own making. This includes the gods of success and wealth and human effort.

As soon as we think of spiritual growth as a list we can check off, then we are falling to pride, because it becomes something that is in our power to achieve.

And that is the paradox that we must become comfortable with. Spiritual growth isn't about right action, it's about relationship. And relationships are never complete. They are always growing.

SPIRITUAL GROWTH ISN'T ABOUT RIGHT ACTION, IT'S ABOUT RELATIONSHIP.

When Jesus answered that the rich young ruler should sell everything, give to the poor, and then follow Him, He was not giving him another list. He was not telling everyone who would read the Gospels for the next two thousand years that they had to live in poverty to follow Jesus. What He was telling the young man was that everything he had done that he was proud of, he had to give up. Even more than that, anything else he wanted to check off his list was meaningless in terms of eternity.

Jesus was telling him that everything he had on earth, every effort, every right decision he had ever made, every dime he'd ever earned, would never be enough to secure a place in eternity. Eternity cannot be bought or earned or won. Eternity must be found. And the only way to discover it is to follow Jesus.

We can do everything right. We can make all good decisions. We can live a pious life and do our devotions every day. But until we realize that relationship is not about earning something but about loving Someone, then we are still working under our own power, and we still have more to give.

Spiritual maturity is not a place we can reach through effort, much to the rich young ruler's dismay.

Maturity is not something you either have or do not have; it is something you grow into. A mature Christian is one who knows they will never arrive at maturity, and they are becoming mature only because they recognize that they are not. It is the humility inherent in the recognition of our weakness that reveals if we are on the path to maturity or if we are simply skipping down the Christian road, hoping that someone else will have found an escalator by the time we reach the next mountain.

CHAPTER THREE

THE EXAMPLE

There is a danger in writing about spiritual maturity because the minute we decide we know what maturity is, it shrinks back a step from where we stand. Like the rich young ruler, as soon as we feel like maturity is something that can be achieved by checking off boxes, we add more boxes that will later need to be checked off.

That does not mean examples are sparse and we need to wander around looking for a starting point. Rather, the starting point is easier to find than we ever thought it might be.

More than that, this starting point is also the finish line. It is the one where you can spend an entire lifetime growing closer and closer to Jesus without ever having to, or wanting to, step over. In fact, once you discover this starting point, everything else tends to fade away in the unexpected simplicity and beauty of God's plan for our relationship with our Creator.

The account of Abraham and Isaac in Genesis is one of those that is both simple and complex, foundational and expansive. It is a narrative that we tell children as they first learn about faith, and it is one that we return to as adults with furrowed brows simply because of the uncomfortableness of the entire encounter between Abraham, Isaac, and God on the mountain.

Abraham has long been considered a "father" of the Church. Even before the modern Church, the letters written by the followers of Christ held Abraham up as an example and as a father of faith. A cursory count reveals that Abraham is mentioned more than seventy times in the New Testament. This speaks to the fact that Abraham's relationship with God is one that has long been returned to as an example of maturity.

Like all the people God used in the Bible, Abraham was far from perfect. When he and his wife first appear, it is with the names Abram and Sarai. He is seventy-five years old, they are childless, and God promises that He will make a great nation of Abram and his descendants.

But Abram cannot make sense of it (he has no children), and Sarai is frustrated, so she takes matters into her own hands and gives him her handmaid, Hagar. After Hagar conceives, Sarai feels that Hagar disdains her for her childless state, so Sarai treats her harshly and the pregnant Hagar runs away into the wilderness. God protects Hagar, and she eventually comes back. Ishmael, her son, is born when Abram is eighty-six.

When he is ninety-nine, God again speaks of His covenant with Abram and changes his name to Abraham and Sarai's name to Sarah. Angels soon visit Abraham and Sarah and tell them she will have a child even though she is far beyond child-bearing years (she is ninety at this time). She does give birth to a son, and they give him the name Isaac.

Here is where we reach the famous part of the story where God tests Abraham by asking him to sacrifice his only legitimate heir, Isaac (Genesis 22:1-14).

This is one of those stories that those of us who grew up in the Church remember, mostly because it is disconcerting. First, it's not fun to think of God testing Abraham. We do not like the idea of our hardships being a test, but the Scripture is clear here, God is, indeed, testing Abraham.

The second thing we sometimes find unsettling is the detail of Isaac's age during this encounter on top of the mountain.

If we go back in time to the days of Sunday school and felt boards, you might remember the cutouts of Abraham and Isaac. Abraham usually had billowing, white hair and a long beard and Isaac appeared as a boy of indiscriminate age, but young.

This understanding is probably due to our own cultural influence as well as a language barrier. The word that is translated as "boy" or "lad" or "youth" here is used in other places in the Bible with the understanding that a "lad" or "youth" is much older than we tend to picture.

In fact, Rabbinical tradition places Isaac's age at around thirty-seven due to the textual evidence that points to this event taking place just before Sarah's death at one hundred and twenty-seven years old.

Additionally, if we look at the other places where this word is used, we know that in the story of Elisha, a "youth" is between twenty and forty years old. Ishmael and Joseph are both called "lads" at around the age of seventeen, and Benjamin is a "lad" at twenty-two.

If we consider clues from the story itself, where Isaac carried the wood up the mountain for his father, it becomes apparent that Isaac is not a small boy. A child could have never carried the amount of wood necessary for a sacrifice.

I think the picture of a young Isaac that we develop is also due to the uncomfortableness of the story itself. It's hard to wrap our minds around an adult sacrificing a child, but we can make it happen if we imagine Abraham telling Isaac to close his eyes and with Abraham carrying the full emotional burden of that awful decision and Isaac remaining innocently unaware.

But if we lean into the discomfort, a much deeper story comes into focus.

For starters, we must remember the book of Genesis is all about how things went wrong, and how God chose one family—the line of Abraham—to try to get things back on track. We also must remember how Genesis works within the redemption story in the rest of the Bible. Abraham's line is Jesus's line. After the fall in the opening chapters of Genesis, everything that happens through the rest of the Bible is part of God's plan of redemption for the earth.

When we read the story of Abraham and his descendants and we read about how he lied and made huge mistakes and how God still chose to call him righteous because of his faith (in Genesis 15:6) even before this awful test, we begin to develop a picture of a God who loves creation and humanity so much that God works within our own brokenness to bring about our salvation.

But God asks him to sacrifice his only child. On the outside, this seems little more than confusing at best, and at worst, cruel. From outside of the entire story, it makes no sense how a God who is good could ask a parent to sacrifice their child.

Here, though, God is not only asking Abraham to sacrifice his only child. He is asking for so much more. And that is where the incredible picture of faith comes into focus. God asks more of Abraham than his child because Abraham's child was the promise that God had given to Abraham. That child represented answered prayers and a promised role in God's redemption plan.

Abraham held a promise of God, the covenant that God would use him and his family and that his descendants would number like the stars; however, like us, Abraham had to learn lessons before this could happen.

The first lessons were the simple ones that we all must learn. Do not lie. Do not cheat. Do not have a child by your wife's handmaid. And the temptation—once we think we have a handle on these things—is to think that we understand God's role in our lives.

This is backward, a mature Christian understands that our life has a role in God's plan not the other way around. God does not fulfill a role in our lives, our lives fulfill a role in God's plan.

GOD DOES NOT FULFILL A ROLE IN OUR LIVES, OUR LIVES FULFILL A ROLE IN GOD'S PLAN.

Learning these first lessons makes us feel mature, even to the point that we tend to consider those around us who live a good life to be mature in their faith. Which is why we ask for "meat" instead of "milk" and why we look at the older lady in the pew and think that she is probably a mature Christian. But this is not maturity in faith. This is good behavior. There is an element of maturity in it, but basically, it is a formula for best results. Simple obedience, while an important lesson in our spiritual walk, is not faith.

Abraham carries a promise, like we all do since the resurrection of Christ: God has made a way for us to be involved in the redemption of creation. We have a purpose.

Now, knowing our purpose doesn't mean our view of what is happening is God's view. For Abraham, that meant God had promised him a son, so, with the understanding that Sarah was barren, Abraham and Sarah took matters into their own hands and Abraham had a son through Hagar.

This wasn't God's plan, though. This was Abraham looking at the problem with human abilities and paving a way for a divine promise to be achieved. It's a hard lesson to learn, and one that we could draw a million parallels to even if we only consider the past few years.

For Abraham, though, their interference in God's plan made Sarah miserable, and while the Bible does not chronicle Abraham's emotional state throughout the conflict, it couldn't have been easy for him to watch the disruptive and destructive results of his folly.

Abraham learned the first lesson—to behave. The second one was more difficult—believe. Believe that God has the power and the wherewithal to make happen what God promises in God's timing and resist the temptation to use questionable human solutions to resolve a situation that will take supernatural involvement.

If it's God's promise, it will come about through God's provision.

Really, this second lesson is one in humility. We are not in control, and we must be okay with that.

Again, it is not an easy lesson to learn, but once we do, then we can begin to grasp that being a follower of Christ, and dedicating our lives to God, means more than following an instruction book. It means more than the letter of the law. It means accepting our new identity.

After Ishmael is born, Abraham is given a new identity. For Abraham, it was a literal change in name. For us, our new identity is shifting out of the sense that we are alone, that what we do does not matter in the big scheme of things, and accepting that we are a child of God, with all the responsibilities that that title carries.

Then the final lesson.

Abraham learned to behave and to believe—both lessons we must learn—but then God tested Abraham in a way that makes us exceedingly uncomfortable, because in this test, God not only demanded that Abraham behave and believe, but also that he demonstrate the depth of his belief.

Think about it this way: When Abraham walked up that mountain, he walked with a beloved son, who was the only answer to the promise that God had made to him. And when Abraham took that knife, and was willing to sacrifice his son, not only was he willing to give up something that any parent would agree is of immeasurable value, but his faith in God was so strong that he was also giving back to

God the only way that God had created to fulfill His covenant with Abraham.

And this is why Abraham's example is considered a cornerstone of faith. This is why when we look for examples of mature faith we turn to these ancient pages. When Abraham raised that knife, he wasn't just sacrificing what he loved, he was sacrificing what was promised to him. He was telling God that he loved God and trusted God even if he could not see the path to the fulfillment of God's promises.

How many of us can say that our faith is so strong that we are willing to give God back the promises He gave to us? Or has our spiritual walk stalled at simply standing firm on those promises?

We spend a lot of time in the Church talking about standing firm on God's promises, but Abraham's example makes it clear that the path to maturity is more about having enough faith and humility to let them go.

And this understanding goes against everything we are taught by our culture. Culture tells us to stand our ground, to demand what is ours, to be brave and bold and know who we are. We have watched this play out again and again.

But God's culture says *trust in Me*. Know that God has it all under control. And as evidenced through Abraham, believe to the point that you give the promise God made to you back as an offering.

If we return to the idea that Isaac was old enough to understand what was happening, then we begin to see a beautiful and unexpected picture of fulfillment develop.

Isaac was old enough to overpower his father. Isaac was old enough to ask and understand why his hands and feet were being bound. Isaac would have heard the stories about God's covenant with Abraham and God's promise to make Abraham's descendants as countless as the stars in the sky. Isaac knew his role in all of this.

It didn't matter, though, because Abraham's faith was so strong, and Abraham's example was so solid, that Isaac, also, chose to play a role in all of this. Isaac, along with his father, was willing to remove himself from the only equation that they could have seen to play a role in God's story.

Abraham's faith was in a place where instead of celebrating God's unconditional love for him, he was demonstrating his unconditional love for God. Abraham passed the test.

And the result of this is a picture so complete, so beautiful, that the evidence of God's hand on this story cannot be mistaken.

You see, the mountain that Abraham and Isaac climbed was part of the same range as the one Jesus climbed. Isaac carried the firewood; Jesus carried the cross. The lamb that was provided for Isaac's release was discovered in a thorn bush. The Lamb of God wore a crown of thorns.

Is the picture taking shape?

When God tested Abraham, he went head-to-head with Abraham's earthly expectations of what redemption would look like. Face-to-face with Abraham's expectations of his promised role in all of it. And when Abraham gave it all up, God sent the lamb.

Abraham's test of faith was a precursor to the test of faith all of Israel would face when they made the choice to crucify the King who didn't meet their expectations, the King who didn't look or act like a king. It was a test that Israel didn't pass.

And now, Abraham's test of faith can be seen as a precursor to our own.

Is our faith strong enough to accept Jesus for the gift that He is, or do we try to reshape Him into our expectations? Is our faith strong enough to accept God's plan or do we have to understand what that plan will look like?

IS OUR FAITH STRONG ENOUGH TO ACCEPT JESUS FOR THE GIFT THAT HE IS, OR DO WE TRY TO RESHAPE HIM INTO OUR EXPECTATIONS?

How have our actions in the last few years evidenced our faith in God's sovereign reign?

Are we holding back, waiting for the Messiah to be the one who looks like victory, the one who looks like prosperity, the one who looks like winning, or are we willing to hold our hands out like Isaac did, are we willing to watch them be bound, are we willing to give up any role we thought we might have and sacrifice it for the one that God has?

Will we stop at standing on what we see as the promises of God, or will we step over them, leave them behind, because they are not as valuable as God Himself? Will we still worship even when it seems like there is going to be nothing but us and God?

This is why we look to Abraham to find an example of what Christian maturity looks like. Because his relationship with God went beyond obedience, beyond simple belief, past hoping for and standing on the promises, and journeyed into a place where he loved God back.

It's a lesson we will all learn. Even if we never discover how to love God back here on earth, this completion is part of the plan. God is the God of grace. We will love God back. The line of redemption that strings from Adam and Eve, through Abraham and Isaac, through Jesus, comes to fulfillment when the elders who represent us cast their crowns before the throne of God and sing that God is worthy (Revelation 4:10-11). We will demonstrate our unconditional love for God when the elders take every reward, every promise, every symbol of their accomplishments, and give them to God because the fruits of their accomplishments are not even a shadow of the gift of simply being in God's presence.

But I want to learn how to love God back now. If you do too, this is where we start.

CHAPTER FOUR

LOVING GOD BACK

After linking spiritual maturity to loving God, how we demonstrate our love to God is the next question, but the place where we can start is almost too easy to dwell on. And maybe this is one of those assumptions that pastors made in past decades that increased the Church's vulnerability. We assumed that the Church knew the value of the Church.

In retrospect, however, we may have underestimated the number of people who were sitting in the pews out of habit or compliance, those whose journeys had taught them how to behave and believe but stopped there. Maybe we underestimated the number of people who joined our congregations simply as a social club. But with nearly half of our brothers and sisters reporting that they are not that enthusiastic about returning, it is obvious that many of our people have been attending every Sunday for the wrong reasons. If we are maturing in Christ, we are learning to love God back by loving what God loves—humanity and the Church.

The fact is, it's impossible to separate the call to love God from the call to love others and the Church.

> IT'S IMPOSSIBLE TO SEPARATE THE CALL TO LOVE GOD FROM THE CALL TO LOVE OTHERS AND THE CHURCH.

Jesus came to fulfill what the prophets said. Jesus came to redeem what had been lost. Jesus came to pay the debt we could never pay. All the while He traveled, taught, performed miracles, and loved people, He was preparing His disciples to carry His message to the corners of the earth, creating the Church.

Thankfully, Christ's directive did not hinge on the perfection of His disciples. Quite the opposite. The group of people who He had the most difficulty with were those who lived the most "*perfect*" existences—the Pharisees.

Instead, Jesus habitually chose the weak, the flawed, and the humble to spread His message. Jesus chose broken people because they are all He had to work with, and our brokenness is the exact problem He came to resolve. Jesus chose people like Peter—a man who denied knowing Jesus, and the same man who Jesus claimed was the rock He would build the Church upon—to take the most important concepts ever communicated and spread them to the rest of the world: God loves us, cares about us, has a plan, and we have a role.

The Church, for all its challenges, is the bride of Christ. Ephesians 5:25-27 reminds us that "Christ loved the church and gave himself up for her, in order to make her holy by cleansing her with the washing of water by the word, so as to present the church to himself in splendor, without a spot or wrinkle or anything of the kind—yes, so that she may be holy and without blemish" (NRSV).

Together, we work for and watch for the fulfillment of prophecy and the restoration of creation. The Church is primary to the plan that Jesus implemented. To think that we can be Christians and forsake the Church is folly.

We are meant to be in relationship with others. We long for communion because we were made in the image of God. We long for God because God longs for us.

To love God is to love His Church. And learning to love God back is the starting point for seeking spiritual maturity.

BOTH/AND

> "Tell me how much you have entered into
> the suffering of those around you, and I
> will tell you how much you love them."
> ~Martin Niemöller

Living in community is difficult, and we are not always good at it. We are slaves to our culture, to our history, and to our own broken explanations of why things are the way they are. In the United States we are brutally individualistic. This is great for seeing our sin as a personal responsibility, but perhaps not the best worldview for demonstrating mercy for the weak and the hurting. Often our churches reflect this.

It took a year in seminary for me to finally understand that communion was about more than individual recognition and remembrance of Christ's sacrifice for me. The focus on Christ's death and my own sin wasn't wrong, but it also wasn't the complete picture. There's more. I learned that taking communion is about community and identity and forgiveness of others (especially those in the Church) so we can begin to understand the sacrifice that Jesus made for us. I had to learn that just because I knew something to be true in one way (largely because of my culture and upbringing) did not mean it can't be true in other ways. Much of spiritual growth is learning that spirituality is not the either/or environment we thought it to be. Rather, it is both/and.

God both loves us and disciplines us. God both watches over us and allows us to walk in freedom. We can love others and have expectations of each other. The list is endless.

This past year we've taken some hits, and there is only one honest explanation for the seats that remain unexpectedly empty. Our people are scattered because they stopped actively growing in love with the Church.

Those of us who are left must ask ourselves why.

Why is it that people have decided their lives are better without the community of those who share their beliefs?

Is there a lack of understanding on their part of the importance of church? Or has the Church done something that makes the community less useful than we like to think it is? Those on the inside point to a lack of maturity and understanding on the part of those who left. But if the plethora of articles, blogs, and videos are any indication, those who have left are pointing to a lack of maturity and understanding by those who remained. Maybe it is both.

Maybe it is a both/and situation rather than an either/or.

Maybe those of us who remain must humble ourselves enough to consider the possibility that we have made some mistakes.

CHAPTER FIVE

DEFINING THE PROBLEM

If we consider the possibility that both those who left and those who remain have room to grow, then those of us who are still sitting in the pews need to listen to the reasons that our absent family members are giving for their exit—without becoming offended.

In Ephesians, Paul reminds us that "our struggle is not against enemies of blood and flesh, but against the rulers, against the authorities, against the cosmic powers of this present darkness, against the spiritual forces of evil in the heavenly places" (Ephesians 6:12, NRSV).

We need each other to grow closer to God. We need the challenges; we need the encouragement. Spiritual growth does not happen in isolation from other believers. Even the monks in monasteries devoted to silence and time alone with God live in community with others who share their longing for closeness to Jesus. We are fooling ourselves if we think that the Enemy will not use our own righteous indignation to continue to chip away at those relationships.

Our dedication to humility and to being willing to place love before the need to be right—by not insisting that our decision to remain proves we are on higher moral ground—is the only way forward.

As it would happen, we do not have to look long or hard to find the reasons. A glut of articles, videos, and blogs have been popping up ever since the pandemic that speak to this issue. It is heartbreaking to realize that those who left have done so with enough interior conflict and hurt that they are telling us outright how we need to fix the problems they see.

Their reasons vary from social to practical to political, but the one thing they have in common is that disagreement is at the core. This is a spiritual issue, a basic misunderstanding of the fact that God wants us all: all our differences, all our uniqueness, all our experiences. God uses us all because of our different perspectives.

We struggle with this in the Church. It's easier when we begin with a foundation of similar ideals and beliefs and move from there. But we must remember that even Jesus rejected this desire for simplicity in His own small group of leaders. Jesus chose both Matthew, a tax collector, and Simon, a zealot, to be two of the twelve disciples. Tax collectors in Jesus's time were universally hated by the Jewish community for their collusion with Rome. Jewish leaders considered it a sin to pay taxes to anyone but God. Zealots were Jewish nationalists whose fanatic views made them willing to suffer for what they viewed as the purity of the Jewish faith and the rejection of Roman influence and laws.

Jesus willingly chose both men to be in His most trusted circle of friends. They lived together, traveled together, prayed together, ate together, healed the sick together, and after Jesus returned to heaven, they both worked to spread the truth of the gospel.

Because God's truth surpasses our own.

The gospel is bigger than our political ideologies. The gospel is more important than if we are for or against Rome. It is miles ahead of the question of our backgrounds or experiences or anything else that shaped the way we perceive the world in which we live.

The problem that we are dealing with today is this basic: it is a lack of appreciation for those who may think or behave differently. If we want to have effective ministries, we must do better than this. We need to follow Christ's example and learn to love and depend on those whose views are different than our own.

We need to realize that Jesus chose both sides for His team. To alienate the side that disagrees with your perspective is to weaken your ability to spread the gospel. Knowingly weakening our abilities to spread the message of the cross in preference for our own comfort is, basically, sin.

> TO ALIENATE THE SIDE THAT DISAGREES WITH
> YOUR PERSPECTIVE IS TO WEAKEN YOUR
> ABILITY TO SPREAD THE GOSPEL.

THREE CAMPS

This book is written for three groups of people.

First, it is written for those who have left the Church. For those who, through recent struggles, have found solace in a faith that echoes the sentiment in Emily Dickinson's poem number 236:

Some keep the Sabbath going to Church—
I keep it, staying Home—
With a Bobolink for a Chorister—
And an Orchard, for a Dome—
Some keep the Sabbath in Surplice—
I, just wear my Wings—
And instead of tolling the Bell, for Church,
Our little Sexton—sings.
God preaches, a noted Clergyman—
And the sermon is never long,
So instead of getting to Heaven, at last—
I'm going, all along.

I don't think there is a single Christian who does not

feel some resonance with this poem. Church is hard. Praising God for creation and beauty is not. There are many days when we walk out of our houses on a Sunday morning, hear the birds and feel the breeze, and would like to keep walking instead of getting into the car to pile into an air-conditioned building and smile at the same people who were more than happy to challenge our perspective on social media earlier in the week.

But there is a flaw here. While this is a beautiful poem, Dickinson has fallen into the either/or trap that so many of us have on occasion. The truth is, we should be making time to walk through the natural cathedral of the woods and give God praise for the gift of the trees and scurrying animals. It should not, however, come at the expense of gathering with believers so we can learn to be more effective in the ministries that God has called us to.

Going to church was never meant to fulfill all our needs as Christians. Going to church is supposed to be our challenge and our refuge when things are difficult. If you have left the Church, this book is for you. It is to remind you that the body of Christ is supposed to be a safe place to ask the hard questions and to learn more than the trees can teach you. And if your old church is not this place, then find one that is. We need to love the Church like Christ loves the Church, and we need to learn from the Church like the Bible admonishes us to do. If you can't do these things in the church where you grew up, then, with the leading of the Holy Spirit, and with prayer and fasting, move on to a place where you can challenge and be challenged.

If you can't find that place, consider the possibility that God is calling you to shine as a beacon in the place that feels dark to you.

The second group of people this book is intended for is those who are tired, those who have fought the fight, listening to the arguments on every side. This book is for those who love the Church and are perplexed by it in equal measure—for those who understand why the first group left, so they feel somewhat hypocritical standing in the path of their exodus because, if they are honest, they don't really blame them.

This group of people has stayed. Maybe because of habit, maybe because they are optimists. Either way, they know that the answer to the problems of the Church lie in the Church. They are not ready to give up on their foundational belief that the Church is the bride of Christ, and they are called to be part of the story.

Finally, and perhaps most emphatically, this book is written for those who are still sitting in the pews, confused, hurt, and angry at those who have left. This group does not understand what has happened, and maybe even explains the departure of their brothers and sisters as some sort of spiritual failing on the part of those who are now missing.

And this might be so. The Enemy will use any means available to weaken the Church and people leaving their church family is absolutely a win for the wrong team. If we do not take a step back, though, and examine any possible role we might have in their departure, is this another avenue for the Enemy to claim a win?

Is the fault entirely theirs? And if not, do we even care? Or do we only want the brothers and sisters back who conform to our ideals?

In other words, are we Pharisees?

A CALL FOR HUMILITY

When there is conflict, there is only one way forward if we want to address it biblically. Colossians 3:12 reminds us: "As God's chosen ones, holy and beloved, clothe yourselves with compassion, kindness, humility, meekness, and patience" (NRSV).

At the most basic level, this means we must listen to what others are saying and respond not defensively, but with an open heart. If we are offended, we must ask why this offends us, and push our answers further than justifying our own intolerance with biblical support. That each of the three groups listed above love Jesus is assumed. If you are reading this book and have never pursued a relationship with Christ, then there are other books with which to begin. The reason for this is that the solution must begin somewhere, and here it begins with the assurance that the brothers and sisters who have left love Jesus and the brothers and sisters who remain love Jesus, and both continue to desire to play a role in the vision for redemption of all creation. Including ourselves.

The problem is, we can't respond with humility unless we truly value the person who challenges us. This cannot be a pride-laced value based on deluded ideas of superiority where we choose to tolerate their wrongness because we benevolently see them with the potential God sees them. Rather, this is a true appreciation of them because their perspective causes us to examine our own and makes us more fit for Kingdom work.

Finally, James 1:19-20 leaves us with yet another point to ponder: "Let everyone be quick to listen, slow to speak, slow to anger; for your anger does not produce God's righteousness" (NRSV).

Pause and let that sink in. Our anger—whether we have left or remain—does not produce God's righteousness. You, I, and those around us, cannot move forward believing that our conclusions are morally superior to the conclusions of a person who might have completely different life experiences than we do. We are never the distributors of God's righteousness. Adam and Eve made the mistake of desiring to define good and evil instead of trusting God's justice. Let us not repeat the error.

All correction, therefore, must be robed in humility. Without this, we'll never find the starting line.

CHAPTER SIX

A CHANGING LANDSCAPE

Before we can deal with the reasons listed for the exodus by those who have left the Church, we must grapple with a difficult truth: Our world has changed, and this is frustrating for many people who have remained in the Church.

Anyone who has been in the Church for any time at all knows that the Church is typically behind a decade or two when it comes to cultural shifts. This comes from our tendency to be rather narrow-minded, and in the Evangelical Church, to build our lives around our local churches and their events, classes, and services. It is not uncommon for many of us to make at least two trips to our church every week, and if we are in leadership, often more.

That means that our lives consist largely of our families, our jobs, and our churches.

We also tend to limit any negative moral influence from movies, shows, music, and other media, so when shifts happen in the outside culture, they often go unnoticed by much of the body of believers for some time.

This isn't all bad. The Church acting as a family who cares for each other and is interested in each other's lives is not outside of what the Church should be doing. But it isn't all good either. When it comes at the expense of us building relationships with those who need Christ, we must admit that there is room for improvement.

Likewise, when it means that we panic when we finally realize what is happening outside of our chosen realm, it signals that there are some underlying problems with how we connect to the world that God created for us to live and work in.

Recently, I was listening to a high-profile pastor as he spoke to a huge audience. At one point, at the beginning of his sermon, he mentioned that it feels like the culture here in America is turning against the Church. The crowd mumbled and applauded their agreement.

What he said really bothered me. It's not that what he said wasn't true. Culture has undoubtedly turned against the Church. Organized religion is, for many people, something they barely tolerate. Prayer isn't practiced in schools unless initiated by the students, and we no longer, as a nation, begin meetings and important events by looking heavenward and reminding ourselves that we are not the biggest, most important thing in the world.

Our culture, just out of habit and practice, used to remind Christians and non-Christians alike that there was a bigger picture than our own cares and concerns. That we were created for a purpose. And I think, as Christians, we came to expect this kind of support.

That pastor's sermon recognized this change. He wasn't wrong in his assessment. I just question the value of us staying in that place of discontent with our culture simply because it does not reflect Christian values.

That world is gone. The outside culture does not support any view that puts any concern over that of the individual. Everything is now about "me."

Unfortunately, it isn't only the people outside of the Church who struggle with this influence. Even Christians are falling prey to this cultural drive to think that our own convenience is the most important thing, and our habits are affecting our families and our churches.

We keep our kids out of Sunday school because they want to sleep in, but then we wonder why our Christian kids seem just as entitled and impatient with anything that doesn't have an immediate benefit that they can feel as their non-Christian peers.

We attend Sunday morning services when it's convenient, and we don't spend time seeking God in prayer and reading our Bibles, and then we wonder why God feels so far away. We knowingly choose to put our own calling on the back burner, and then we wonder why we are sad and rudderless.

We don't volunteer (one of the main ways we get to know people and build relationships) and then wonder why we don't feel connected to others in the Church. And we loudly complain about the inconvenience of living in an increasingly secular world but are confused when that same world isn't attracted to the Church.

Tragically, we fail to engage with our own shortcomings when our own members, dissatisfied with a religion that feels like just another commitment, slip away from the body.

If we examine our culture, we are undoubtedly fighting an uphill battle. The outside culture used to remind us that there was something bigger than our own desires. At Christmas, schoolchildren sang songs about Christmas. At community meetings, opening in prayer reminded us that we were brothers and sisters before we began to argue about where Steve wanted to put his fence, and every Sunday, families chose to go to church because they were raised to believe that there was something bigger that we all belonged to.

But we can only get that from the Church now. Without the support of the outside culture, we have to rely on this right here. On our family. On the Church.

I understand the mourning. I understand the feeling that we are trying to do more with less because we *are* doing more with less. It's harder than ever to keep our eyes on the hope that God offers because we aren't getting constant reminders from everywhere and because the culture of "me" is infiltrating even the Church to an alarming extent.

As a pastor, I share the frustrations of living in a culture that doesn't value the Church, because at the same time, the ones who don't value the Church are longing for the kind of community that takes selfless living to achieve.

It makes no sense.

It's like we are surrounded by thirsty people, but they don't believe that the water we hold in our hands will satisfy. This isn't a new feeling though.

Jeremiah 2:13 describes this kind of ancient blindness: "They have forsaken me, the fountain of living water, and dug out cisterns for themselves, cracked cisterns that can hold no water" (NRSV).

I understand mourning for a time where prayer was encouraged in schools.

What I don't understand is when we allow that longing for a time past to get in the way of our future mission. I don't understand how we spend so much time lamenting the way it was—because it isn't that way anymore. I don't understand the anger, the frustration, and the feeling that so many Christians are throwing up their hands because they only see a problem when God is plainly giving us an opportunity.

Here's the question at the very foundation: How can we effectively spread the message of the gospel if we are more preoccupied with our struggle than we are with our calling?

How can we spread the truth if we resent the ones we are trying to reach?

We're called to look ahead. We're called to meet the needs of the present and to live with a vision to the future.

> HOW CAN WE EFFECTIVELY SPREAD THE MESSAGE OF THE GOSPEL IF WE ARE MORE PREOCCUPIED WITH OUR STRUGGLE THAN WE ARE WITH OUR CALLING? HOW CAN WE SPREAD THE TRUTH IF WE RESENT THE ONES WE ARE TRYING TO REACH?

If Jesus walked into your church right now and sat down and talked to you, I don't think He would be asking you what it was like back in the day of the tent meeting revivals.

Instead, I think He'd be a little more preoccupied with what you're doing now for the people out there who have absolutely no idea what it means to walk on this earth as an image-bearer of God. I think He would be more concerned with how you are reaching others with the humble message of the cross—living out His reordered Kingdom where the last are first and the poor are rich—than He would be about learning your perspectives on what it was like when it was easier to be a Christian, when even your culture reminded you that God was there.

So, when I heard that preacher express the same frustration that I've heard from others in the Church so many times before, I was overwhelmed with the feeling that we have to do better. We must be more resilient than this. We need to be in a place where when we look out there, we see what Jesus sees—a world full of people who live every day with the tragedy of not knowing why they were created.

THE OPPORTUNITY OF A SECULAR SOCIETY

The temptation is to think that what we are facing is new. Looking to the Bible, though, helps us see that the problems of those who are trying to live a life of mission are ones our ancestors have dealt with before.

If we look to the book of Jude, we will see that Jude lived at a point in history where Christianity was new. He served the gospel during a time when the Christian message was actively spreading outside of the Jewish community into the secular world. This required that the Jewish ministers—who had grown up learning Scripture, had a solid foundation of knowledge, knew the history of creation, the fall, and of God's longing to reconnect with humanity and Israel's responses and their failures and finally the Messiah who brought resolution to the entire story—had to figure out how to communicate all of this history with the Roman world, who had no idea that God had stepped in and made a way for them to become part of an already running story.

And I can't help but connect that with our own increasingly secular society. The task in front of us might look like foreign territory, like a completely new landscape, but we're not without a map. It's a temptation to think that our experience is unique, but the early church walked the same path that we're walking right now.

You see, the church Jude addressed had a problem that we have today—false teachers had slipped into their midst. The church of the time, filling up with new converts who didn't share a life defined by Jewish law—one that understood holiness is worship, and sacrifice is service to God—the church of this time, because of their lack of knowledge and identity, was vulnerable to false teachers.

And these teachers used God's grace as a justification for immorality. The church addressed in Jude's letter had the opposite problem of the churches that Paul had been previously dealing with. For Paul, one of the main issues was legalism, which makes sense for an audience that was at first, largely Jewish. But for this church, it was a lack of law—largely because the church was reaching a secular people who did not know or value the old teachings.

Does this sound familiar? In the New Testament churches, they had a problem of congregations that were either legalistic or they refused to tackle the topic of sin.

It just goes to show us how flawed we are in our human attempts at balance. If we don't go off the rails in one way, accepting every sin, we'll try to go the other way and condemn everyone who doesn't meet our expectations.

With God's direction, we must find a middle ground. So, we turn to Jude verses 17-23:

> "But you, beloved, must remember the predictions of the apostles of our Lord Jesus Christ; for they said to you, 'In the last time there will be scoffers, indulging their own ungodly lusts.' It is these worldly people, devoid of the Spirit, who are causing divisions. But you, beloved, build yourselves up on your most holy faith; pray in the Holy Spirit; keep yourselves in the love of God; look forward to the mercy of our Lord Jesus Christ that leads to eternal life. And have mercy on some who are wavering; save others by snatching them out of the fire; and have mercy on still others with fear, hating even the tunic defiled by their bodies" (NRSV).

The plan Jude lays out here is one of balance. It contains four very condensed pieces—the first three call the church to holiness, and the last one tells the church how to help others reach salvation. If we take these to heart, we'll be well on our way to understanding how to be a force for God even in a world—especially in a world—that does not know God at all.

JUDE'S PLAN TO BUILD ON
THE FOUNDATION

First, Jude calls on the church to build on the foundation of apostolic faith.

The beginning of verse 20 reads: "But you, beloved, build yourselves up on your most holy faith" (NRSV).

Notice how he calls the church "beloved." In fact, it's the second time he uses the endearment in the last three verses.

I don't think we can skip over this. He's calling those who have fallen prey to the false teachers "beloved." He is calling those who have caused the church challenges and problems, "beloved." He is not calling them out angrily. He is not condemning their blindness. In fact, what he did in the previous verses was cite three Old Testament prophecies, a prophecy from ancient Jewish texts that are not included in our Bible, and the words of other apostles in order to help these new followers of Christ understand their own place in the story.

You see, these new believers didn't all grow up Jewish. They didn't all know who they were. They had accepted the message of the cross, they believed in Jesus, but they didn't have the kind of foundation that would keep them from making errors in judgment, and when people came in with false teachings, these believers were vulnerable.

How many times do we see evidence of this today? How many times do we see high profile preachers with huge followings preaching cheap grace and setting up churches that are little more than social clubs? Preachers who trade discipleship for flashy programming. The problem is, like the Romans who were converted, modern day people who aren't discipled, who don't know their own history, are easy victims for charismatic leaders who are busy building their own kingdom, who sound good and look good but who lack the depth needed to build the kind of church that can thrive and grow and make disciples even when it isn't easy.

But Jude's response to this infiltration is unexpected. Instead of getting angry, instead of trying to fight these false teachings with loud letter writing, Jude calls those in the church who he rightly sees as victims of false teaching "beloved," and then he does write a letter, and uses that valuable parchment and ink to tell them their history, and to teach the new believers and remind the old of where they came from and where they are headed.

Building on the foundation of apostolic faith is building on knowledge and mission. Knowing the "most holy faith" means studying from the apostolic teachings of those early Jewish believers who walked with Christ, who understood the revolutionary plot twist of a Messiah who is all-powerful because He was crucified.

Jude manages to look at those who have fallen prey to false teaching and rightly places the blame on their lack of knowledge, and then takes it one step further, emulates his humble Savior, and instructs with love.

This isn't always an easy task, especially when the false teachers are so loud and held in such high esteem. But Jude makes it clear that we can't abandon the requirement to remain Christ-like even when we are speaking messages of correction.

Like the early Roman Christians, the people who are now coming into the Church most likely have no idea of their history. They didn't grow up in a society where even non-Christians sang Christmas songs steeped in Christian theology. They didn't grow up with church and Sunday school attendance being something that you just did.

Unfortunately, it is becoming increasingly apparent that even those in the Church lack knowledge of their own history. Biblical illiteracy is a term that has been tossed around for a while. I guess we are finally seeing the effects of that lack of understanding in our churches.

This changes the map for how we witness both to those who have never set foot in a church, as well as those we thought were part of our families.

PRAY IN THE HOLY SPIRIT

Our second piece of the plan is found in the second half of verse 20 where Jude calls on the church to "pray in the Holy Spirit."

I don't think that as a church we can stress this enough.

The Christians of this time were living under the influence of Rome, and because the Roman society was heavily influenced by the Greek society, early Roman Christians were greatly influenced by the Greek culture of argument and persuasion. This cultural understanding determined how they navigated their world to a significant extent.

Much as it still does for us today.

Before I became a pastor, I was a part-time high school English and history teacher for a Christian school. At the same time, I was also a college instructor in English and rhetoric at a secular institution. And the experiences I had in these positions gave me an unexpected glimpse into the spiritual problems that arise when we diminish the instructional value of the Holy Spirit for that of the Greeks.

There were all kinds of students in my college classes, and you could tell that some of these students had come from Christian homes. And these students, raised in Christian homes—sometimes having attended Christian schools or sometimes having been homeschooled—were usually well-versed in how to defend their faith.

Well-meaning parents and teachers, who wanted to make sure their kids could compete with the logical push of the secular university, did their best to give their kids an argument for every argument against Christianity that the university might provide.

The problem is you can't argue someone into the Kingdom. And while apologetics might be valuable in certain arenas, it does not have the keeping power of the Holy Spirit.

By the end of the semester, many of these kids who started out as Christians, who were trained in apologetics and the logical principles behind their beliefs, were requesting to write their final papers on topics like "science versus religion," with the winner being science.

Now don't get me wrong, I love science, and I love a good discussion about what science has given us and what it promises for us in the future. I just don't think it makes any sense to try to compare it to religion. I don't have to choose one or the other. But these kids thought they did have to choose because when they got to college, some of their arguments took a beating, and the training by the adults in their life who favored the explanations found in Greek tradition over the mystery of the Holy Spirit resulted in their reliance on logic over Spirit.

But it's the Holy Spirit who speaks to us, who keeps us, and it's our experience and encounter with God that shapes who we become as we pray and seek God.

WAIT FOR THE MERCY

The beginning of verse 21 gives us the third element, and the NIV renders this portion of the verse beautifully: "Keep yourselves in God's love as you wait for the mercy of our Lord Jesus Christ to bring you to eternal life."

The question is, with all the conflicts, with the challenges of living in a secular society—one where we can no longer count on the local townships to help us keep the

Sabbath by closing their stores—how do we stay in love with God? How do we maintain this focus? How do we communicate the gospel better for both those inside and outside of the church?

John 15:9-10 makes it clear how we are to keep ourselves in God's love: Jesus says, "As the Father has loved me, so I have loved you; abide in my love. If you keep my commandments, you will abide in my love, just as I have kept my Father's commandments and abide in his love" (NRSV).

And 2 Peter completes the circle: "But, in accordance with his promise, we wait for new heavens and a new earth, where righteousness is at home. Therefore, beloved, while you are waiting for these things, strive to be found by him at peace, without spot or blemish" (2 Peter 3:13-14, NRSV).

In a time when people's identities were wrapped up in the idolatry of their own lives—when people had no idea that there was something else out there and that they were loved and valued not because of what they did but because of their identity as a child of God—they rocked the world with the message of the cross. In a time where the society was secular, an entire community of people (the Church) changed the history of the world. This community—who lived by principles of faith, hope, and love, who rejected the need to defend their beliefs and simply lived them out, and who walked with the Spirit and lived Christ's gentle example even to the point of martyrdom—this community of people knew that living with this new identity in mind was the greatest witness of all. They never expected their culture to reflect their Christian values.

You see, a church of individuals living out the call to a life of faith, hope, and love is more powerful than any government support. You loving your neighbor is more of a witness than the stores remaining closed on Sunday.

And we need to stop using a lack of support from the outside culture as an excuse for our failure as a witness.

WE NEED TO STOP USING A LACK OF SUPPORT FROM THE OUTSIDE CULTURE AS AN EXCUSE FOR OUR FAILURE AS A WITNESS.

We need to embrace the fact—demonstrated by our own history—that God's Kingdom is not reliant on the support of humanity's kingdoms. We are to live in the love and mercy that foreshadows the coming Kingdom, and when we do that, there is no power on earth that can stop Jesus's message.

HAVE MERCY

While we are depending on our history, our prayers, and dedicating ourselves to demonstrate love and mercy, verses 22-23 contain the fourth and final element in our plan to understanding how we can be a force for God in a world that does not know God at all. The verses read: "And have mercy on some who are wavering; save others by snatching them out of the fire; and have mercy on still others with fear, hating even the tunic defiled by their bodies" (NRSV).

Now, there are 25 verses in the book of Jude, and this is the first time—verses 22 and 23—that Jude takes the time to discuss how the church is to act regarding the false teachers. That in itself should cause us to pause. The first 21 verses have to do with personal holiness. The first 21 verses, in a book that is primarily about false teachers who have infused the church with the ideals of their secular society, speaks to individual responsibility rather than rails at the church, or worse, the outside society.

As Christians, we can't escape the fact that our primary responsibility is our walk with Christ. That what we do and who we choose to be does not change regardless of what comes against us. The call to carry out our duties as an image-bearer of God should be our focus.

Our expectations as Christians are a constant because God is a constant. No matter our culture—the time we live in, our struggles, or our victories—the call to be holy and true to our identity as Christians, does not change.

That does not mean when there are struggles that we just stick our heads in the sand. Jude does eventually look toward those who are causing the problems and directs the church's attention to them. But he also does this in an un-expected way.

He doesn't tell the church to close ranks and take on a defensive stance. He doesn't have to.

People who are built up in their faith, who are empowered by Spirit-led prayer, and who love God do not have to be defensive. They're walking in holiness. They have received grace, so they offer grace. They're children of the Most High who cannot be swayed away from their identity and what that identity demands. They are living toward God's vision of the future, they know the battle has been won, and they know that their responsibility is first, to holiness, and when they attend to that, their next step is to help others find the saving grace of Jesus. These people know that there is nothing that draws others to Jesus like being like Jesus, being filled with grace and hope and assurance, not being afraid of the future or distracted by what is going on around them because those living for Christ know that the battle has already been won.

They are living in the balance between caring for God's creation and looking heavenward, because they have come to the realization that they can't fulfill one without the other. If the quest for holiness draws them into legalism, then they are no longer seeking holiness. If the quest for heaven makes them so distracted that they can't be Jesus to the surrounding community, then they are not seeking holiness.

So, instead of dealing with false teachers like we might expect, Jude calls for mercy for three specific groups of people.

First, he calls for mercy on "some who are wavering."

Who are those who are wavering? Most likely these are the people who have fallen under the influence of the false teachers. They are the ones who have been led astray. They are the sheep that need to be brought back into the fold—not through argument, not through threats of isolation from the rest of the church, not through anger—but through mercy. Brought back in by the Church acting in their gentle and humble identity as followers of Christ. You see, nothing, nothing, is more attractive than mercy. Nothing makes us want to belong more than witnessing grace at work.

Next, Jude calls the church to "save others by snatching them out of the fire."

This refers to a group that is in more danger than the first, and Jude chooses to use the language of the Old Testament to get this point across. Here, he turns to the prophets, Amos and Zechariah, and uses language that recalls their warnings to a straying Israel. In this part of the verse, Jude is telling the church to bring back the ones who have strayed—not only the ones who are wavering in their faith…and the way to bring them back is also with mercy.

The last group that Jude requests mercy for is "others with fear, hating even the tunic defiled by their bodies." In other words, those who are facing the consequences of their sin. The church's response to these people, the ones who have been marred and marked by their sinful choices, is again supposed to be that of mercy.

Now, this leaves us with the question of what to do with those who want to be in the Church and at the same time embrace their sin—people who call themselves Christians yet fail to attempt to live to Christ's example. It's a challenge that is very applicable for today.

Jude doesn't answer this directly, and I think there is a reason for this.

Jude seems to have high expectations for the Church. Jude calls the Church to walk a very narrow path. He asks that we live holy lives while, at the same time, extending grace to others. Of course, the practical steps that Paul lays out for us need to be followed by the Church leadership whenever there is conflict or when we experience false teachings, but Jude's solution is a personal one. His solution is for every individual in the Church. His solution is about bringing the Church closer to God when we face these kinds of challenges, and then letting that holiness be a testimony.

And this is interesting, because if we are living holy lives, I think that maybe we can't do anything but extend grace.

If we are truly living holy lives, then don't we have to see the world that Jesus came to redeem for the opportunity that it is, rather than a threat to our way of life?

CHAPTER SEVEN

GOD'S PLAN STANDS

One evening after school, one of my daughters came home and casually mentioned that she'd been reading the Bible aloud to a friend on the bus for the past month.

That got my attention. When I was a kid, I'd have probably been shoved in a locker for doing something like that. But I didn't grow up in a completely secular society. In the 80s, we were turning secular, but we weren't there yet. And there's a big difference between what sharing Christ looked like then and what it looks like now.

I asked her how that started…how it was that she ended up reading the Bible aloud, off an app on her phone, on the bus to one of her friends.

She told me she had been staring out the window on the bus one day, and a girl who was sitting next to her asked her if she was praying. This girl's family was from India, and she had no understanding of Christianity. She just thought my daughter looked like she might be praying.

My daughter responded that she wasn't praying at the moment, but she was a Christian. That got them talking, and this girl was curious, so they decided to start reading the Bible together on the bus.

You know the interesting part? Over the weeks, the kids in the rest of the seats around them had become very quiet.

The rest of the kids had started listening.

That's when it hit me. They're listening because for them the stories are new. They're different. And the adults and teachers and mentors in their lives may have decided that they are bored with the stories, but for these kids, this is something they had never actually heard.

We live in a secular society, and these kids don't know why they were created or who Jesus is or how we can live with purpose and hope or how we are part of the huge story that spans all of history and calls us to be part of the solution to suffering and brokenness.

You see, when we send our kids into schools that don't promote or initiate prayer or read the Bible, we are now sending them to people who haven't rejected Jesus because they've never heard about Jesus. Not the real Jesus, anyway.

That's the opportunity right now. They might have heard teachers and comedians make fun of religion, and they might have heard their parents explain that organized religion is a farce, but they've never heard about Jesus.

It used to be we were surrounded by people who had either accepted or rejected Christ. Now we are surrounded by a growing number of people who have never been offered that choice—even in our churches.

This is why, when I hear the Church's frustration at a culture that doesn't agree with their values, I cringe a little. Because if we are impatient, if we are angry, if we think we have the right to expect unbelievers to live by Christian standards of holiness, then we're not being Jesus to them. We're not living out the plan that the leaders of the first century church—the church that spread exponentially despite their secular society—laid out.

Jude tells us in verses 18-21: "In the last time there will be scoffers, indulging their own ungodly lusts. It is these worldly people, devoid of the Spirit, who are causing divisions. But you, beloved, build yourselves up on your most holy faith; pray in the Holy Spirit; keep yourselves in the love of God" (NRSV).

Jude tells us to expect the problem of false teachers, of an infiltration of ungodly perspectives, but his response is not to get angry or upset or see this as a failure of the Church. His response is for God's people first to be concerned with their own holiness, and then extend grace to those who have fallen away.

And when we do that—when we act like a church who knows who we are and what we stand for and when we act like a church that is not threatened by what is happening out there, when we extend grace by listening and responding—then we are doing what we are supposed to be doing.

It is then, like the first church, that through the Holy Spirit we will draw people to the Church or even back to the Church. Because the message of the cross is irresistible. The message of grace and hope brings people in. We must trust that God has this all under control.

Because He does.

LISTENING

Matthew 18 is quite clear about what to do in the Church when someone is wronged. The biblical response to conflict is for the one who feels like they have been sinned against to speak with the person who offended them. If that does not work, they are to bring one or two witnesses into the conversation. If there still is no resolution, the answer is to bring it to the Church, and if an unrepentant heart still prevails, they are to be excused from the company of the Church.

What happens, though, when the Church doesn't listen?

What happens when the questions have become so large, and the refusal to answer them so universal, that there is no one left to ask?

Thankfully, those who have begun the exodus have not remained silent. And while it is tempting to fall into the trap of rejecting these issues as an attack on the Church, there is a call for those who remain to see these questions for what they are—questions. Almost daily, and unfailingly, with every new crisis from the pandemic on, whether that be in the realm of racial reconciliation, access to medical care, political upheaval, or another mask requirement update by the CDC, people on every area of the spectrum have been exceedingly vocal. It is not a surprise that after isolation and situations that are out of our control, we express little patience for the feelings that accompany the sense that our opinions have not been heard.

For too long in the Church, one's faith has been judged as strong or weak by his or her level of confidence. If you look like you have it together, and you sound like you know what you are talking about, then you must have a strong faith.

In many cases, those who are deemed the most "mature" Christians have earned that status because of their willingness to put on blinders and plow through the questions, sweeping aside the uncomfortable or incomprehensible for the relative safety of easily harvested pat answers and biblical clichés. This agrees with our generally bullheaded, American response to most challenges.

But it does not leave room for the deeper "why" questions that must be asked if we want to truly grow spiritually.

Remember, Abraham first came into alignment with his behavior. Belief was next. The third, was the difficult one: demonstration. The first two were the easy ones.

Abraham had to demonstrate his love for God. We do this by loving what God loves—in this case, Jesus's bride, the Church.

Here is the place where it all intersects: The spiritually mature response when people leave the Church is to demonstrate our love for them by listening to their concerns because, if we are honest, we all have the same big questions.

Our faith tells us that Jesus's example is the answer to every human difficulty, but the Bible is more than an instruction book for best results. The human experience requires more than a list of rules. This is why Jesus taught with parables. If the answers were simple and not matters of relationship and discovery, then Jesus would have simply told us yes and no for every situation.

But spiritual growth is not simple. It is relational. It is messy. And if you are tempted to answer complex questions with self-assured sound bites and then categorize any follow-up questions as a lack of faith, simply put, you are part of the problem.

What if those who have left the Church did so because the people who were there have abandoned their own search for spiritual maturity?

WHAT IF THOSE WHO HAVE LEFT
THE CHURCH DID SO BECAUSE THE PEOPLE
WHO WERE THERE HAVE ABANDONED
THEIR OWN SEARCH FOR
SPIRITUAL MATURITY?

What if the exodus is due to a lack of spiritual maturity on the part of both those who left and those who have stayed?

LISTING THE PROBLEMS

> "The person who knows only his side of
> the argument knows little of that."
> ~ Karl Barth

Again, we do not have to dig too deep to discover the reasons people have left the Church. They have been vocal about it, so we have a starting point. And because we suspect that our relationship with the Church and with others in the Church is a matter of both parties' spiritual maturity, these specific objections can and should be categorized as spiritual challenges.

After reading countless articles, scouring social media sites for #exvangelical, #deconstruction, #religioustrauma, #exfundamentalist, and talking with my pastor friends, it seems the problems people are listing as reasons they have left the Church can fall into three main categories:

1) Problems within the Church structure, practices, and leadership

2) Challenges in navigating the nexus between our culture and our faith

3) A longing for what was, rather than living in the vision of what can be

Now the hard part. This is the chapter where you may be tempted to snap the pages shut and ask for a refund because this is the stuff we do not want to hear. These objections are the ones that caused you or someone you know to blast out on social media. These arguments are the ones we are tempted to simplify because they are easier to deal with. But these challenges are more complex than that, and simplifying and stopping the conversation devalues the question, and more importantly, the spiritual journey that demands the questions…and the answers.

The first questions are those that deal with church leadership, and because they prick our pride and question the things we love, they are especially difficult to listen to without making an unthinking response that diminishes the seriousness. While you may or may not agree, the charges are as follows:

The Church refuses to engage with questions about biblical interpretation that threaten strongly held ideals.

The Church has rejected science but embraced superstition.

The Church has failed to empower women.

The second group of questions have cropped up out of the confusion created when our culture has infiltrated our churches, which is ironic, because we constantly talk about the problem of the culture's influence on our churches. This, though, demonstrates that the line between what is cultural tradition and what is a biblical mandate has blurred. These challenges, which often coincide with financial motives and greed, include:

The adoption of secular measures for success within the context of the Church.

The perpetuation of celebrity culture in the Church.

In cases of abuse, the Church has often chosen to protect leaders over the victims.

Finally, the third group of questions that those who have left are asking are based in idolatry, making gods of our ideals and our own traditions. These indictments are founded in our failure to live toward the future that God has envisioned, rather than living in the here and now. The complaints of those who have left often take the shape of:

The rise of Christian nationalism and the idea that those who worship together must share political ideals.

The choice to ignore the voices of those who have experienced oppression. This includes deprioritizing the concerns of those who suffer in poverty and diminishing the records of those who have experienced racism.

CHAPTER EIGHT

FIRST THINGS FIRST

The list of problems communicated by those who have left the Church is a difficult one to accept, and you have probably already been listing the reasons to argue the points that you assume the rest of this book will make. After all, it is part of our culture. We want to be right. We want our answers easily understandable and simple to communicate. We like to win by sound bite. And we like to camp on a point of view and defend it.

I want to pause, though, because we need to lay the foundation not for how we will argue whether these charges are worthy of their inclusion; rather, we need to lay the foundation that being willing to engage with these topics is a matter of spiritual growth and maturity—both for those inside the church as well as those who find themselves on the outside. We need to look at these as a challenge to our mandate to love the Church. We need to look at these from all perspectives and see if we can understand why someone—other people who share our love for Christ—may not agree with us.

We will not argue for or against the problems listed above that people perceive within the Church. There are any number of resources that argue for or against any and all of these topics. For me, one of the biggest topics is the question of female leadership in the Church. There are mounds of books written on the subject, and as a female pastor, you can probably guess where I stand. But I will not dedicate the pages here to an attempt to prove that Jesus's teachings have made space for me to fulfill the role that I do in my Church. I want to dig deeper.

Because the problem isn't that different perspectives exist. The problem right now is the division caused by those on either side thinking they know the only possible answer.

In short, the problem isn't what we want it to be: one that is easily solved if we could all just agree with whatever our favorite, or at least the loudest, person in the room believes. Rather, the problem is the lack of unity caused by the assumption that we should all be agreeing about every topic.

But until heaven and earth has been completely redeemed and humanity is once again reflecting the image God created us to reflect, we will not agree on every topic.

So, the danger isn't in our agreement or disagreement. It is in the disunity caused by the disagreement.

Until we are finally restored, our understanding will

be imperfect. Everyone's understanding will be imperfect. That is why we need each other. That is why we are all branches grafted onto the vine of Christ (John 15:5). That is why some are the hands, and some are the feet (1 Corinthians 12:12-27). We need all our experiences so that we can be effective in the true reason we are on this earth—to reflect the image of God.

THE DANGER ISN'T IN OUR AGREEMENT OR
DISAGREEMENT. IT IS IN THE DISUNITY
CAUSED BY THE DISAGREEMENT.

INTERPRETATION AND EXPLORATION

When God first created humankind in the garden, the earth they shared was one of perfection. There was no sin. There was no war, no destruction, no evil. This is because they relied and trusted God to define good and evil. They lived in the paradise of God's complete justice.

Then Adam and Eve decided that they wanted to define good and evil on their terms. This changed everything because humanity is not capable of this all-encompassing view. Humanity does not have the God-like perspective it takes to comprehend complete justice in all situations.

Still, God met humanity where they were at. God made a covenant with the Israelites that made them active participants in the redemption of the earth. But the Israelites failed to live up to the calling.

Their ancient culture was a brutal warrior culture. We only need to read into the first book of the Bible to see that there were things acceptable in their time that would never fly now.

This raises some challenges for modern, Western readers. Our temptation is to read the Bible as if it was written only for us to read. The problem is it wasn't. Rather, it was written as a record to read and learn from, and it expresses things that may or may not be directly applicable to modern believers.

Let me explain. There are places in the Old Testament where it is recorded that God told the Israelites to go to war and leave no survivors—including women and children, young and old. In some places they were even instructed to cull the animals. This does not mean that God wants us to go to war with our enemies now and indiscriminately slaughter. What it does mean is that God knew the Israelites would not be able to keep their eyes on God and their covenant with the distraction of constant attacks, ruthless societal pressure, all the while contending with the influence of foreign gods.

God was providing brutal instruction for survival in a barbaric world.

We no longer do this. Not because we don't believe in the Bible or in the application of God's Word, but because we now live in a world that places those who commit war crimes on trial. Even with our limited abilities of justice, most of us do not live in a warrior culture, and we have grown beyond the need for our God to command decimation in war because as Christians we share in the forward-looking call of God's redemption story.

For as evil as this world feels sometimes, Christianity has had an impact. The freedom inherent in a theology of a loving God who wants the best for creation has changed the earth. In a world of inequality and hierarchy, Jesus was the only Savior to reach in with the revolutionary message that those who had been downtrodden and marginalized are the first in God's Kingdom. And through Christ, we have become active participants in God's plan for this planet. As such, we have the ability to read the Bible with the knowledge that the demands God made on the Israelites were not universal demands for all time.

The reason this distinction is important at the very beginning of our discussion of challenges and questions that the Church is facing is because we first must accept that there are differences in interpretation of God's Word, and we have to accept that no one interpretation is perfect. There is a reason that Jewish scholars have been debating the Scriptures for thousands of years—the words of God are complex and applying them is a moving target. For any one person to say that they have the complete understanding of every controversial topic because they feel the Bible is on their side is arrogant at best. No one can see that deep into the mind of God.

Thankfully, we do not have to.

Because our spiritual journey is one of discovery.

We begin here, at the place of unknowing, at the place of humility, and with the understanding that it is this admission that starts the path to maturity. In this place, we ask God to reveal to us what we need to learn.

It is necessary that we place the desire to know God in a deeper way above the need to be right about God's words. Maturity requires that we step away from the certainties that have undoubtedly been tainted by our culture and habits and trade in our need for a strict interpretation of Scriptures for one that simply longs to fall deeper in love with God. Not through compliance. Not through rules and regulations. Not through our strivings. But through relationship. Through understanding. Through embracing some of the paradoxes and letting them open our eyes to the perfection of Christ's sacrifice and the resulting call on our lives.

We must set aside all our assumptions and frustrations so that we can fall back into love with the imperfect thing that God loves: the Church.

Think about it this way: Outside of the Church, are the people who you look up to as examples of maturity the ones who think they know everything and will die on the hill of their choosing to defend their point of view? Or are they the ones who listen, consider the opinions of others, and then make room for those who hold opposing viewpoints to still share in the conversation?

We need to make room for people to explore.

In many circles, this journey has recently earned the term "deconstruction," and like with each new buzz word, a whole host of pastors and teachers have risen up against what they see as a dangerous trend in the Church.

I understand this term, though, and it doesn't offend or even concern me. You see, as the Church, the temptation when we hear of "deconstructing faith" is to understand it as "demolishing faith" because the group of people who are using this term to describe their journeys are calling into question ideas and perspectives that we might have always held dear.

That's not what they are saying, though.

If we listen closely to the stories of those who are "deconstructing," we can hear a group of people who inherently understand that the term "deconstruction" implies that there will be a rebuilding. If we listen closely, we will hear a group of people who often still love Jesus, and who are trying to apply Jesus's teachings to their broken worlds.

As the Church, it is our duty to help guide these seekers on their spiritual walk rather than become offended that their walk might look different than our own.

Our first duty as the Church is to fight the temptation to dismiss those whose experiences have led them to different conclusions, and instead learn how their lives have led them to stand in a place that we do not stand.

Our first duty as the Church is to have a faith that is strong enough to stand up to the questions. We can't move forward and continue to serve the world if we stick our heads in the sand every time we face a challenge that might call into question the way we view our world. Thank God that the gospel we love is far more expansive than our own imaginations.

THANK GOD THAT THE GOSPEL WE LOVE
IS FAR MORE EXPANSIVE
THAN OUR OWN IMAGINATIONS.

CHAPTER NINE

ENGAGING CRITICALLY

When someone walks up and shares that they don't like this or that about the Church, the message the pastor preached, the way the children's ministry is structured, the fact that the Bible study doesn't cover the topics that they want to delve into, or any other criticism, our temptation as a people who happen to like the church, the pastor, and who happen to be friends with the kids' ministry team is to feel a little ruffled.

After all, it isn't like we can't see the reasons for their critique, it's just that we fear the questions will lead us down a dangerous path.

At least, that's the excuse we give.

But we must entertain the possibility that our hesitation to give credence to the critical mindset has less to do with protection than it has to do with our pride. Here, I want to pause, though, because there is a difference between looking at something critically so we can find places for improvement, and outright criticizing something or someone.

As Christians who hope to change the world with the message of the cross, we need to be honest and willing to admit that we do not do everything perfectly. If we are being truthful, this is something that everyone struggles with both inside as well as outside the Church.

It seems like inside the Church, though, we find ways to spiritualize our hesitation to admit that we are not perfect.

If we happen to like the way things are going, if our teenagers love the youth pastor and seem to be growing in their own walk with Jesus, and if we are teaching a Bible study about one of the topics that the person who is questioning things doesn't appreciate, then their critical comments are probably not welcome.

However, if we dig in to why they are not welcome, at the heart of the issue, it's not because we are protecting the Church or spreading the gospel message, it's often because we are prioritizing our experience over theirs. Plain and simple.

And that's pride.

We might have a million very good reasons not to want to engage in the criticism of what we love…but it's still pride. It's still us before them. It's still an unwillingness to have our perspective called into question.

This discussion hits home for me in a very personal way. As someone who grew up in the Church, and as someone who God created to question everything (apologies to my elementary schoolteachers), I always felt like I had no place in the Church—at least no place where I could be my real self.

Simply put, the Church doesn't like a critical eye. It makes us uncomfortable. And growing up, I could never understand why, when I pointed out something that didn't make sense, I would be dismissed and my concern soundly ignored. It wasn't until I was older that I could understand that in the Church, questioning the status quo is the same as indicting the status quo—that questioning itself was a dangerous first step to dismantling what some people have come to love and depend on.

I didn't realize that the Church's refusal to engage concealed the festering truth that arrogance and pride and a sheen of certainty are very useful when we are trying to convince ourselves that we are the mature ones and that we are right.

For me, the things I do not question are the things I do not care about. I love God. I care about the Church. So, I constantly felt like in order to be in harmony with the community of believers, I had to ignore the things that didn't make sense.

For a long time, I did just that. I shelved the questions and chose shallow harmony for the sake of remaining in the Church.

I ignored the things that didn't line up.

I listened to people say things that didn't sit right, and I kept my mind tightly reined in and my mouth closed.

After years of training, I came to the place where I understood that blind acceptance was the safest route to keep peace in the Church.

Then, I came to the place where I realized that that peace was at the expense of my own calling.

God created each of us to interact with our world in a way that is unique, and after years of fighting to suppress what I had been made to feel were the parts of me that were a danger to the Church, I had fallen into the trap of helping to create the environment of sameness that is now what I see as contributing to the exodus of people from the Church.

For that, I am sorry.

I am sorry that I kept my mouth shut when I should have spoken up, that I ignored the erroneous slippery slopes and straw men arguments, that I stopped listening to my own heart under the pressures of the Church.

Now, we have come to a crisis point. With so many of our people scattering, citing experiences that echo mine, we no longer have the luxury of sitting in our comfortable chairs and convincing ourselves that the Church is right and they are wrong.

Because I know they are not always wrong, and the Church is not always right.

The Church makes mistakes. Pastors and leaders and

priests and teachers and lay people who love Jesus are human, and we all make mistakes.

THEY ARE NOT ALWAYS WRONG, AND THE CHURCH IS NOT ALWAYS RIGHT.

It's time for us to set aside our pride and open our hearts to truly listen to our brothers and sisters who used to be in fellowship with us.

You may have strong feelings about one issue or another. That's okay. I am not asking you to change your mind or lower the standards you feel God has set before you. I'm only asking you to consider that someone who might not agree with you can also be useful in the Kingdom of God.

I'm asking you to consider the possibility that there are more than two sides to every argument, and that the third side is our relationships with each other.

I'm asking you to see people first when you are tempted to see issues that appear to be either right or wrong in your mind.

It is maturity at work when we seek a foundation to work together rather than look for the things that keep us apart and ineffective.

There is still an entire world full of people who don't

know the freedom in a loving God. There is enough work for all of us to do.

In seminary, I met a Presbyterian minister who was led to a relationship with Jesus by a homeless gay man.

If we allow it, God will use us all despite what others may see as our failings.

As a Church, let's rejoice in that truth and move forward together.

BIBLICAL INTERPRETATION

The litany of complaints from those who have left the Church began with questions about biblical interpretation. This is intentional, because it seems to be the one that always crops up in the middle of any of the other arguments. While we will not spend time refuting or debating the individual issues, this one deserves a place at the head of the discussion, because it is the one thing that has been used, despite the issue, to consistently shut people up when they say things we don't want to hear.

Here's what it looks like: One person states an opinion, another counters, and then they both come up with verses to support their views.

Inevitably, they end up pointing out why their interpretation of any given Scripture is the best.

Then there is a stalemate, and two (or more) of the family of God are now dug in and willing to die on whatever hill they chose.

This is where the failure takes place. It isn't in the fact that there are two different perspectives. It's in the fact that there is now a rift in the relationship, and we are now less capable of doing what we are called to do as a Church.

Frankly, if one person wants to believe a literal interpretation of seven, 24-hour days of creation, and another wants to read the creation event in a more figurative light, is any harm done by allowing the brother or sister room to consider their chosen interpretation?

Does it hurt the Church to allow someone room to explore?

The argument is imperfect. All our arguments will be, because we are imperfect. I wasn't there at the time of creation, and neither were you. But I am here now, and, looking around at the hurt that exists in the world, there is evidently enough work to be done for all of us. There are enough widows and orphans (James 1:27) who need to be served.

I do know one thing. When time comes to give an account of what I have done on this earth, I do not want to be the one standing there, justifying why the Church was ineffective in winning people to Christ because "those people" didn't believe in the same interpretation I did.

There is another danger present, though.

We are all on our own individual faith journeys. The walk will look different for each of us. I sincerely hope that twenty years from now, my path has led me to a place where my perspectives and understanding about God has changed from where I am right now.

The problem is, if I must camp in one spot and defend that stance, I allow no room for my own personal growth. I also allow no room for growth in the person whom I happen to disagree with at the time.

While I might think I have the best argument for a literal or a figurative interpretation of the creation account, in defending my stance I have now created division between believers and while doing so stifled both of our abilities to grow in our walk with Christ.

Can you see the pitfall? If I take pride in my own understanding, I sacrifice the work that needs to be done. Whereas if I make room for those with different interpretations and focus on the mission rather than the obstacles in the path of that mission, we can do the work we are called to do.

The added bonus is that we will be acting as the Church, in love and unity, and the mission becomes easier. People are attracted to harmony. When those who should be—by all earthly understanding—incapable of unity are instead moving together for one goal, we are exemplifying the restored relationship that echoes back from our redeemed future. This is what moves the Church forward. This is what speaks to a broken world. This is what draws people to the truth. This is the power that cannot be corrupted...unless we allow it to be.

DUST ON THE TABLE

I once was talking to a nutritionist about a diet I was trying out. I asked her about things like ketchup and other sauces and if those were okay to include in my plan. She deemed that they were "dust on the table," and then went on to explain that if a house is burning down, we don't go around dusting the tables.

The comparison of my personal health to a burning house notwithstanding, the phrase has stuck with me.

How often do we look at the issues we have in any area of our lives and focus on the minutia? How often are we standing in a burning building, dusting tables?

When we have almost half of the Church not excited about being part of the Church anymore, I think it is time to admit that the building is burning.

And many of us are still dusting tables.

We must ask ourselves why.

Maybe it's because the problem is too big, so we focus on the details instead.

Maybe it's because we've always dusted tables, and we're so used to it, so we haven't bothered to look up and see what is happening around us.

But I suspect, if we are honest, even if the other two reasons are true, maybe we like dusting tables.

Maybe it makes us feel useful, productive, and like we're adding value.

The problem is, now there are people standing on the outside looking in, shouting through the glass for us to look up, and we're so intent on what we are doing, that we don't even notice the house falling in around us.

The reality is, in the Church, we like our lives. We like our churches. And we like doing things the way we have always done things. We take pride in what we have built, in what we have cared for, and the criticism coming from outside is not wanted.

We want things to stay the same, and we would rather argue to try to convince those outside to value what we value so that we can keep on doing the same thing.

But they've stopped listening.

And so we sit, proudly dusting our tables, having the same conversations, complaining about the "outside world" in the same way we always have, and lamenting the fact that there are fewer and fewer of us dusting the tables.

This is sin.

There is no other way to say it.

Placing our own interests, our own habits, our own practices ahead of the priorities that Jesus set before us is, in a word, sin.

PLACING OUR OWN INTERESTS,
OUR OWN HABITS, OUR OWN PRACTICES
AHEAD OF THE PRIORITIES THAT JESUS SET
BEFORE US IS, IN A WORD, SIN.

We must look toward heaven. We have to see what is above us so that we can do what has been placed before us.

LORD OVER ALL

> "A Proud man is always looking down on
> things and people; and, of course, as long
> as you are looking down, you cannot see
> something that is above you."
> ~C.S. Lewis, *Mere Christianity*

Before Paul met the Lord on the road to Damascus, he was a religious man. In fact, his lifetime of training, his achievements, his knowledge of God's Word, his duty to his culture and the tradition of the Pharisees, made him a leader of leaders.

He protected his synagogue.

He defended his beliefs.

He spoke out against heretics.

He preserved tradition.

He resisted change.

He opposed those who threatened to sway his people with the temptation of a false Messiah.

A Messiah who was not the kind of king they expected.

One who dared to question the Pharisees.

One who favored relationship over knowledge.

One who healed on the Sabbath.

One who ate with sinners.

One who failed to be impressed with the Pharisees' knowledge, interpretation, achievements, and dedication to duty.

Because Jesus is about relationships.

Jesus is about restoration.

It only took one encounter with Jesus for Paul to change from someone who killed Christians to the one who would teach the Church how to be the Church.

> IT ONLY TOOK ONE ENCOUNTER WITH JESUS FOR PAUL TO CHANGE FROM SOMEONE WHO KILLED CHRISTIANS TO THE ONE WHO WOULD TEACH THE CHURCH HOW TO BE THE CHURCH.

One moment of truth for him to see every conflict in a different light.

Over the past few years, as I watched lifelong friendships implode over politics (or fill-in-the-blank on the topic of the day), I couldn't help but notice how like the Pharisees we all acted.

When someone spoke out against a practice that those in the Church held dear, they were dismissed, and the Church, the earthly reflection of the Kingdom of God, gladly sacrificed relationships for the power of being right.

God forgive us.

FLABBERGASTED

As I began writing this book, I started speaking with other pastors and friends who have been in the Church for most of their lives. I explained that I wanted to write about falling back in love with the Church, about loving what God loves, and about how the current environment where people are leaving because they are not being heard while others are watching, labeling their departure as a moral failure, has exposed a lack of spiritual maturity for all the parties involved.

It surprised me to learn that many were astonished that I would think that the decision to leave the Church was not simply a failure on the part of those who left.

Consequently, I tried to explain with examples—with the list of problems that those who have left have stated.

The one response I fielded over and over when faced with the list was incredulity.

The people I talked to in the Church: a) did not believe that the things on the list were really that important; b) wanted to know my stance on the issue and then proceeded to debate from there; or c) didn't care because the people who left should have understood that the Church has certain immovable stances on things and that's just the way it is.

I was flabbergasted, and for a while I stopped writing.

This was because I wanted *Back to Church* to be about

choosing relationship and the duty that all Christians share to show God's love to the world over topics of contention.

I prayed over this, sought out more conversations, and realized that until the Church understands what that list represents—until the Church sees themselves *in* that list—all talk of relationships and love and care and justice are lost.

When I make the claim that the Church has adopted a celebrity culture, those reading this book need to be able to see this in action for any real change to start.

And maybe your church is the furthest thing from celebrity. Maybe you are in a tiny rural congregation, and the idea of your ancient pastor sporting a pair of ripped skinny jeans because he wants to look more "relatable" is laughable. That doesn't mean that one of the other claims will not apply.

Not every church will fall into every category (prayerfully!). But I think that we can place ourselves in the shoes of our brothers and sisters who have maybe tried a few churches and found various challenges within those congregations. After all, every church will have problems. Where it becomes a crisis is when we fail to admit it and instead go into defense mode rather than a repentant mode.

When the people outside of the Church call those inside the Church hypocrites, I do not think it's because they expect us to be perfect. The hypocrisy comes in when we claim that we are all sinners who are saved by grace, and then we defend ourselves against anything that would hint that we have done something wrong, while failing to extend grace to others.

The reason that people have left is a matter of maturity—theirs and ours. Theirs because they do not see the necessity of Christian community, and ours because of two reasons. First, we failed to disciple them well enough that they understood the essential role that community plays in a Christian's life; and second, because the reason that we haven't discipled them well is often tied to our own pride, greed, and idolatry.

CHAPTER TEN

PRIDE

> "For pride is spiritual cancer: it eats up the
> very possibility of love, or contentment, or
> even common sense."
> ~ C.S. Lewis, *Mere Christianity*

> "Earnestness is not by any means every-
> thing; it is very often a subtle form of
> pious pride because it is obsessed with the
> method and not with the Master."
> ~ Oswald Chambers

Pride belongs here in our conversation because it is our pride in our own understanding that keeps us from realizing that we are not perfect. Pride makes us defensive, and it keeps us occupied with the busy work of building fences around what we love, blurring the line between what God has instituted and what we have understood.

When we begin to mistake our own efforts on behalf of

the Church for God's efforts, criticism sounds like an attack on our very belief system rather than a question about how we, the Church, have chosen to mobilize that belief system.

PRIDE MAKES US DEFENSIVE, AND IT KEEPS US OCCUPIED WITH THE BUSY WORK OF BUILDING FENCES AROUND WHAT WE LOVE, BLURRING THE LINE BETWEEN WHAT GOD HAS INSTITUTED AND WHAT WE HAVE UNDERSTOOD.

It is insidious. Pride allows us to be deceived in multiple ways. First, we think that our thoughts, ideas, and opinions are somehow better informed than others, despite the reality that our set of experiences are completely different than the next person's. Next, because we think that our opinions are somehow better, we put more faith in our decisions than we should. Just because we are Christians does not mean that we see with God's eyes. This is why we pray for discernment. But if we already think that we have the only correct opinion, how much good is that prayer going to do? It does us little good to pray for discernment if we do not do so from a place of humility.

Finally, because we have not drawn strict lines between what God has said and what we, as humans, have instituted in response to God's direction, we defend our creation while thinking it was God's. Jesus instituted the Church, Paul taught us how to live in community as the Church, the disciples demonstrated how the work of the Church was to be done. Jesus did not say that the song service needs to have three hymns or that Sunday school class should start at 9:00 a.m. or that any song that is more than five years old is no longer relevant. But you will find in any number of churches people willing to fight for their hymns or their new songs as if the salvation of the world depended on it.

There is nothing wrong with having preferences, but when we place those preferences on the same level as God's Word, we are disordered.

THERE IS NOTHING WRONG WITH HAVING PREFERENCES, BUT WHEN WE PLACE THOSE PREFERENCES ON THE SAME LEVEL AS GOD'S WORD, WE ARE DISORDERED.

And when we are disordered, people notice. As they should.

SCIENCE AND SUPERSTITION

"God has not the slightest need
for our proofs."
~ Karl Barth

Not that long ago, a woman walked up to me after service to tell me that she had made the decision to leave her other church. This is always a sad statement. Generally speaking, the pastors I know do not like it when someone decides to leave one church to join a new congregation—even if that new congregation is their own. Leaving a church means leaving a family. It means taking your prayers, your time, your talents, and your resources from one vision and finding a new one to invest in.

There is a price that the body of Christ pays for this.

I told her we were glad she joined us for that week, and I asked her what had brought her to us.

Many times, when someone leaves one congregation and goes to another, they never let the previous church leadership know of their intention. Because of this, it's my habit to ask why they chose to worship with us, and if that question opens a door for me to encourage them to have a conversation with their previous pastor, I do so.

This woman was very quick to answer: "The other church decorated their stage with those triangle shaped patio canopies, and of course, triangles are of the Devil."

Lacking anything intelligent to add to this statement, I waited for her to continue.

She didn't disappoint.

I left that conversation shaking my head and realizing that when people say that the Church embraces superstition, they aren't completely baseless.

Now, there might be a million reasons why this woman thought that triangles are evil, and maybe you share her opinion—but the fact that something like triangles made one person leave their church family in search of a new one is the real problem for both the woman and the church she left.

You might think that this is an isolated incident. I implore you to ask your pastor if he or she has ever heard anything like this. They more than likely have.

Everyone has their own lines when it comes to the place they perceive where the world we cannot see collides with the one we can. For this woman, it was demonic shapes. For someone else, it might be Harry Potter or the influence of Disney. For another person, it might be back-masked music. I know people who consider yoga to be evil, and I know others who blame their broken appliances on spiritual warfare.

You may agree or disagree with any or all of that list. It doesn't matter because, whatever it is, if it causes you to see your church family in a negative light, or if you talk about your views so much that others don't want to join your church family and share in your mission to spread the gospel, then it's time to take a step back.

And this pricks our pride.

We all, whether we realize it or not, construct our own realities based on our own justifications, but it's pride to think that others should dismiss their own realities once they have spoken with us. The job of changing hearts is God's. If you think someone's heart needs to change, then the appropriate response is to lead them to Christ, and then let the Holy Spirit do His work.

The real tragedy is that the Bible, Jesus's words, explain this as clearly as possible. John 13:34-35 says: "I give you a new commandment, that you love one another. Just as I have loved you, you also should love one another. By this everyone will know that you are my disciples, if you have love for one another" (NRSV).

Here, Jesus is making it clear that it is not what we stand against that promotes the gospel; rather, it is what we are for. We are for each other. We are showing love to each other. It is that love, and only that love, that communicates to those who have not heard of Jesus's love for them.

It is simply not our task as a Christian to make every person agree with every other person. It is not our duty to convince others that the triangles we think are evil are, in fact, evil. Our only job is to reflect Jesus's love, and we do that through relationships that, without the covering of the Holy Spirit, are inexplicable. Tragically, when we trade love for agreement, it causes disunity and then we are truly less likely to be a beacon of Jesus's love and less likely to bring others into precisely the kind of relationship with Christ that we hope to be facilitating with our opinions.

As far as the science goes—there's not a lot we can do about the outside world thinking that we have rejected science, except to be aware of what science is and what it is not. Science is based on testable hypotheses. We can't test faith like a scientific hypothesis, and I don't think we really want to. This isn't to say we can't study it, apply it, and learn from the world God gave us. It simply means that maybe we should be more concerned with being the light of Christ in a dark world than defending what we think are proven theories from the Bible.

I can scream all the apologetic evidence I want to a room full of people, but at best I will be telling those who follow God what they want to hear and getting eye rolls from those who do not believe. When it comes to this, I can't help but think that if we simply loved people and gave them room to find Christ and then explore the gift of this world once it has been illuminated by the understanding purchased by a relationship with God, then maybe we would have one more soul in the Kingdom that we might not otherwise have had.

I am not saying that apologetics is not valuable. I appreciate it immensely. I just can't find where Jesus ever tells us to argue anyone into the Kingdom.

I JUST CAN'T FIND WHERE JESUS EVER TELLS US TO ARGUE ANYONE INTO THE KINGDOM.

GENERATIONS

I am a member of Generation X. The generation known for being a bit cynical, sarcastic, and generally hands-off when it comes to arguing for our viewpoint.

Generation X grew up sandwiched between the two biggest generations of the last century: the Baby Boomers and the Millennials—generations that have made countless news headlines for their inability to see the world from the other's point of view. Where Boomers see laziness, the Millennials see workaholics. Being part of the generation between the two, I suspect that one of the reasons there seems to be such a divide between the Baby Boomer generation and the Millennial generation (especially in the Church) is because Generation X was so outnumbered that they collectively didn't make the effort to guide the Church into the changes that the larger community was experiencing.

In reality, Generation X was the generation that began the exodus from the Church, but there weren't enough of us to cause much of a ruckus.

Anecdotally, I think there were so many Boomers that my generation didn't think the fight was worth it. So, while many of us left, some of us found a way to work within the system, and the systems, structures, and practices that may have evolved gradually didn't, because the Boomers continued to stay in the positions of authority in the Church that Generation X had abandoned.

This meant that the conversations that should have happened as we went from a modern to a postmodern society went untended, and now we have two generations entrenched in their modern and postmodern camps, refusing to budge.

The price of this clash of worldview is felt deeply by the Church. Here, the black-and-white world of the modernist has collided with the gray reality of the postmodern Millennials, and in many ways, this has resulted in what is essentially a lack of a common language.

For example, apologetics spoke deeply to the modernist Baby Boomers because they are drawn to concrete answers with specific beginnings and endings. For the postmodern Millennials, who are more comfortable with a mixture of a scientific and a supernatural explanation, there is less need for the set-in-stone reasoning that the Baby Boomers desire, and the hyper-focus and need for hard facts makes the Millennials question how true these "facts" really are.

The Millennial generation is more likely to accept a Christian worldview from someone who says "I don't really know how I feel about a literal seven-day creation, but we can study it together" than they are someone who gives an hour-long lecture on why Christians must believe in a literal seven-day creation. Millennials are comfortable with ambiguity in things like spirituality, and they enjoy the path to discovery, whereas Baby Boomers responded to authority and what they understand as absolute truth.

Where Baby Boomers see moral absolutes stemming from reason and law, Millennials see morality as a product of culture, community, and individual values—including faith.

When Baby Boomers, with their bootstrap approach to difficult situations, preach hard work and discipline as a solution to their problems, Millennials, who are drawn to tolerance and service, see the suggestions of Baby Boomers as overwhelming and lacking soul, and maybe even Christian love.

For the Baby Boomer, the role of religion is a private role, but for the Millennial, religion should be a personal choice, beneficial for the community, and never controlling. This is why relationship over reason is what draws Millennials into the Church. By nature, they are distrustful of what they see as the controlling aspects of religion, but hungry for relationship. This is how the Millennial generation can be one of the least religious generations, yet far more spiritual than previous generations.

Thankfully, the message of the cross is a relational message. We simply have to learn how to set aside what we think should draw people to Christ and listen to what they actually need to see from their Savior.

If we want to inspire the Millennials in our congregations, instead of favoring the verses that speak of law, the Church needs to lean into verses that speak of our responsibility to the Kingdom of God and to each other. It is not wrong for the Baby Boomers to prefer law—that preference is a product of their culture and an essential part of the Christian experience. But if we are thinking evangelistically, it also is not wrong for the Millennials to prefer the Jesus who healed the poorest and ate with sinners. This is no less a picture of who Jesus was, and His powerful example for how we are to live is not less important than the verses that tell us how we are to behave.

In 1 Corinthians 9:19-23, Paul reminds us:

"For though I am free with respect to all, I have made myself a slave to all, so that I might win more of them. To the Jews I became as a Jew, in order to win Jews. To those under the law I became as one under the law (though I myself am not under the law) so that I might win those under the law. To those outside the law I became as one outside the law (though I am not free from God's law but am under Christ's law) so that I might win those outside the law. To the weak I became weak, so that I might win the weak. I have become all things to all people, that I might by all means save some. I do it all for the sake of the gospel, so that I may share in its blessings" (NRSV).

This passage speaks directly of setting aside our preferences and our habits for the sake of others. It leaves no room for the Christian to entertain the idea that a lack of common ground is an excuse for a failure to be the Church.

And I'm going to be bold here. The onus is on those who have been Christians for the longest time. The duty to die to ourselves is a duty that has to be embraced by the mature, by the mentors, by the leaders, because new Christians are not going to understand the depths of truth here. The Millennials and the upcoming Generation Z members are the ones the older generations should be guiding, and it is the job of the older, more mature generations to learn their language—not the other way around.

Finding a common language is foundational for us to begin to bridge the gap with those who are concerned with post-modern conflicts like those that deal with the questions of science and superstition. We can't hope to learn from each other if we can't even agree on definitions for these words.

It probably never occurred to the woman with the fear of triangles that someone else might think her perspective a superstitious one. And it might never occur to someone who has piles of what they consider scientific evidence that speaks of a literal understanding of the seven-day creation account that another person may not care, because the story of a Savior who died and made a place for all who suffer is more compelling than any scientific journal.

WHAT CAN WE DO?

1) Search our own hearts to see if there is anywhere we might be harboring superstitions or strongly held beliefs that we use to define our faith.

2) Ask your pastor if he or she has any examples of this.

3) When tempted to get into an argument over these issues with someone, ask yourself whom this serves. Are you following Jesus's mandate to let our love for each other be the primary witness to our communities?

4) Ask yourself if, when meeting with an unbeliever who wants to talk about religion, do you default to trying to "prove" the basis for your faith, or do you rely on your love for that person, on the Holy Spirit, and on prayer to truly listen and discern what will speak to their heart?

5) If you can see yourself in any of this, repent, and remember that true repentance means you make tangible changes in your life.

6) Give thanks to God for using us all even though we are not perfect, and for loving us through our mistakes.

CHAPTER ELEVEN

FAILING TO EMPOWER WOMEN

If you talk to a hundred different women, they will likely give you a hundred different opinions on this topic. The same thing goes for a hundred different men.

Generally, I refuse to argue about women's roles in the Church because I have found that the conversation tends to go nowhere. Until you are called by God to do something that the people who surround you feel like you have no business doing, you will not understand this particular heartbreak. So, this chapter, while it will deal with church leadership and gender expectations, has a very specific goal.

Instead of proving that a problem exists, I want to take the next few pages to highlight how the way the Church has failed to promote female leadership has created a discontinuity that people who live and work outside of the Church are forced to reconcile. Unfortunately, as we can now see, that lack of reconciliation often comes in the form of choosing to leave the body of believers.

To begin, I will tell you about a recent meeting that I attended. It was memorable because it painfully exposed the different realities experienced by women in leadership inside the Church from those realized by women outside of the Church, and it brought into sharp relief one of the reasons why the Church still lacks female leadership.

The meeting was one intended for pastors. Like usual, I was one of about seven women in a room filled with around forty men. It is notable that I am ordained through a church that has never restricted women's leadership—at least on paper.

The speaker was a president from a popular university that many choose to go through for religious training. And as he began to speak, my heart sank.

Through a haze of alpha-male sports jokes, he attempted to connect to the bulk of his audience. After fifteen minutes of verbal high-fives to the males in the room, I realized that this might never end—not the speech, but the problem exposed by his words.

It wasn't that he was purposefully leaving women out—some women love sports. It was simply because the structure, the habits, and the typical practices are so gendered that it excludes anyone who does not easily fall into traditional gender stereotypes and roles.

It's a problem that is being felt by an increasing number of my male colleagues as well. Men who didn't grow up in the church world—who run their households as a partnership, who don't consider it baby-sitting when they watch their own children—sometimes share in the unsettling experience of not quite fitting in to the traditional boxes that the Church is most comfortable with.

We are not talking overt sexism. I don't think that there was a pastor in that room who would have purposefully left me or my female colleagues out simply because of our gender. Instead, it's that we, as a Church, simply don't hear ourselves. We have become so insulated, so wrapped up in our own religious world, that we have not noticed how things have changed outside of it.

Before I became a pastor, I worked in the fields of education and business. When I sat in seminars and business meetings or when I attended continued training as an educator, I never felt like I was an add on—an anomaly that no one really knew what to do with, even if they were okay with my presence.

The problem is that as a female who wants to lead in the Church, they either must pretend to like the sports jokes and/or any other typically male trope that leaders use to relate to their largely male audience, or they have to be very comfortable leading women's groups, which tend to be no less stereotypical than the men's groups.

As I sat in the meeting, I realized that this leads to an even bigger problem.

It's not only about whether women are accepted into leadership.

It's about whether they even want to try using their gifts in the Church anymore.

If we look outside of the Church, we can see that women are leading in all levels of businesses. Their expertise is not simply tolerated, it is actively sought out. Schools purposefully send female scientists into classes so that girls can see the possibilities for their future in the sciences. In children's programs like Girl Scouts or Boy Scouts, leadership development is a priority for both girls and boys.

In comparison, if you look up your denomination's web pages for their girls' and boys' ministries, there is a very good chance that you will see the problem played out quite plainly. The goals for boys' ministries typically include a push for leadership training. They advertise that they are teaching the boys to be "leaders in their church." In contrast, if you visit the page for girls' ministries, the goals are quite different and typically talk about a focus on the girls' relationship with God.

I am not trying to throw rocks here. Both church programs can be exceptional and probably focus on the child's relationship with Christ and their community. But it remains obvious that church leadership is not the goal for our girls.

This is tragic because we can't afford to lose any more of our leadership potential.

If you switch over to the secular Girl Scouts program,

there is an entire page dedicated to the concept that a girl can "be a boss" and learn to be a business leader.

The question this poses for us in the Church is this: If you raise your daughter to know that there are no restrictions on her future, if you raise her in a church that will not limit her ability to follow God's call based on her gender, what clubs are you going to sign her up for to help develop her leadership skills?

One does not have to do complex math to see that we are under serving not only our girls, but also their families as well.

Not to mention the Church.

Coming away from that meeting, one where I had a seat at the table, I was saddened for the future potential for our female ministers. You see, the university president with his fifteen minutes of sports jokes never met the eyes of any of the females in his audience. Until, that is, he got to the last ten minutes, and he started trying to make an emotional connection with a sad story. Then he couldn't seem to manage eye contact with any of the males in the room.

That's when it hit me that it might be too late. You see, I'm one of the minority of people who have decided to stick it out and hopefully see a time when women and men can serve God's people side-by-side.

So many of my sisters have abandoned the hope, though.

I don't think I can stress enough that this is not because males (and just as often, females) are keeping women out of church leadership. I know this is happening in many places, and I am sensitive to the fact that there may be several women who will read this and think I sound like a spoiled brat—after all, I actually have a seat at that table.

There is a nuance here, though, and it is an important one.

After the struggle to win that seat, and then the continued harassment by people who think women should not be at the table, the pressure of conforming to the habitual way that church work is accomplished is, for many people, the last straw.

And this is why so many who have left the Church name the failure to empower women as one of the reasons that they did so.

The Church needs all the leadership ability it can get its hands on. The Church needs strategic thinkers, project managers, theologians—people who can get things done with efficiency and excellence.

THE CHURCH NEEDS ALL THE LEADERSHIP
ABILITY IT CAN GET ITS HANDS ON.

When I go down the list of women I know who are gifted in these areas, can you guess where they are? Not serving in traditional Church roles.

They are the CEOs of corporations. They are entrepreneurs. They have started their own non-profits. They have satisfying marriages where they work together with their husbands as equal partners, or—gasp—they are single... and happy. (The fate of single women in the Church is another topic, but one that also deserves to be discussed.)

Forbes has reported that women are now the majority in non-profit leadership. There is still a gap for non-profit CEOs of businesses that exceed $25 million in revenue, but the tide is turning. As a female pastor, I can't help but wonder if churches had been open and welcoming to their leadership, if churches had actively sought out women to lead, would those women who are now running businesses that serve the community have stayed to serve the Church community, in turn, empowering the Church to make a difference in the towns and cities where they serve?

As I sat in that meeting, my heart sinking with each passing minute, I realized that it is entirely possible that the Church in America might forever continue to hobble along on half of its leadership potential. The Church might never stop squandering the wisdom, the activism, and the balance that female leadership provides.

The Church might just keep on going like it always has been, ignoring its resources because habit and tradition and pride are more important than the message from Jesus that all of us are equally called to bear the image of God, and in doing so, all of us have jobs to do that promote God's Kingdom.

The truth here is that there are a lot of needs in the Church, and we have rooms of girls who love Jesus and who will work for God's mission to spread the hope of the gospel. Will we train these young women to listen to the Holy Spirit even if it challenges our habits? Will we not simply allow them a seat at the table, but make a space for them, so that they do not have to feel like they are fighting against the Church because they want to do God's work?

#EXVANGELICAL

I was mindlessly scrolling through social media, and I happened to stumble into the #exvangelical thread where one woman was discussing the movement to leave the Church and about the heartbreak and pain involved with that decision. What had driven her to make the video I was watching was the need she felt to respond after reading another of the glut of articles by prominent pastors listing reasons why they think people have left the Church.

The author of the article she read listed the reasons as a desire to walk away from God, choosing a life of sin, not wanting to experience conviction, and myriad other reasons that placed the blame squarely on the shoulders of those who have left.

In all fairness, maybe some of that is true. People do leave the Church because they choose to live in a way that they know the Church doesn't condone. The mistake we make is assuming everyone who leaves the Church falls into this one category. The mistake we make is adopting the assumption that is the easiest one for us to adopt—it's all their fault, because that doesn't require anything from us.

Whatever their reasons are, anytime an individual leaves the body of Christ, it should drive us to examine ourselves for anything that might have been amiss with our own practices, habits, and ideas. Instead, it feels like deflecting has become a habitual response on the side of the Church whenever we are made aware of something that we do not appreciate.

For example, when someone mentions the problems they perceive under the heading of racism, ten-to-one, someone in the circle of Christian listeners is bound to bring up the tragedy of abortion.

The truth is, two negative things can and should demand our attention at the same time without one overshadowing the other and being used to dismiss it.

During His time in ministry, Jesus constantly stopped, interrupting His day, to heal the sick and serve those who needed Him. It didn't matter if that person was old or young, poor or rich, Jesus stopped to deal with the issue that was placed in His path. We should be no different.

To put it plainly, it is heartless to respond to someone who is mentioning an issue that bothers them by bringing up another that you think is worse.

We are to be a people of compassion.

Jesus didn't only deal with the problems that seemed more serious than others because every problem is an effect of living in a world where our relationships with God, each other, and creation are broken.

Evil is evil. When we dismiss someone else's concerns, we are telling them that our concerns are more important.

This is pride.

And when we use Scripture to support our redirection of the conversation to what we feel are biblical reasons to do so, we are being Pharisees.

We are choosing law over love.

We are diminishing the needs of another person and replacing them with our own.

Paul was clear that, as Christians, we are to die to ourselves.

In the Church, we must ask if we have strayed from the spirit of Paul's teachings. Are we willing to act in a way that might be unfamiliar or uncomfortable for the sake of the gospel? Or, like the #exvangelicals claim, are we so focused on our habitual finger pointing that we do not even see how our own attitudes and practices can make the Church an inhospitable place?

Before someone gets their undies in a bunch, I am not advocating for loosening our moral responsibilities as leaders in our churches. I am simply reminding us that those responsibilities are often best communicated through example, and in God's timing.

In my dad's church, years ago, there was a woman who started attending after she had found Jesus. I was in high school at the time, and I remember her because I thought she was gorgeous. She also happened to be a new convert, and when she walked into church each Sunday, dressed in her short-shorts and cutoff tank tops, more than a few eyebrows were raised. After all, modesty is a virtue that Christians like to live by.

The women of the church talked to my mom on more than one occasion. They thought that, as the pastor's wife, my mother should talk to this newcomer and help make her aware of what is and is not appropriate attire for church attendance. Thankfully, my mother had enough discernment to tell them to give God time to work.

It took about a year before her clothing choices gradually fell into line with what more people thought were acceptable. But eventually, as she experienced the love of God—which is not dependent on how much skin is exposed and how good that skin looks—she didn't feel the need to draw attention to herself in the same way.

Years later, she married a pastor, and she thanked my mom for her patience, because without that, without giving God time, she might not have stayed long enough to learn the peace and the confidence inherent when we are loved unconditionally by our Creator.

As Christians we are called to be uncomfortable. When we are teenagers in youth group, this often plays out in sermons about being brave enough to be a witness and to tell others about Jesus. As we mature, though, this should change for us.

Of course, we are to be brave witnesses—that goes without saying. But there is a reason that is taught in youth groups. For the mature Christian, bravery takes on a new form: Are we brave enough to look ourselves in the mirror? Are we brave enough to see that the value of being bold, when tempered with humility, allows us to be more things to more people? Maturity demands the kind of self-control that keeps us from expecting others to act in the same way we do, even before they have a relationship with God.

Immaturity looks at others and demands they be more like them. A mature Christian can give grace because they have experienced grace.

A MATURE CHRISTIAN CAN GIVE GRACE BECAUSE THEY HAVE EXPERIENCED GRACE.

WHAT CAN WE DO?

1) Go to your favorite social media page and type in #exvangelical. You are going to run into a lot of hurt, a lot of anger, and a lot of misinformation.

You will find raunchy jokes and a bucket full of the kind of language you do not allow your kids to use. I am hoping that you will also find heartbreak and a whole new group of people to pray for. Please do not respond on the social media platform. You have not earned the right to speak into a stranger's life, and because of this, your words will probably only do more harm than good. Instead, put that energy into doing something positive in your own community.

2) Listen, listen, listen to your kids when they bring up issues that are important to them. If your kids go to public school, they probably have perspectives on issues that you don't agree with, and you don't even know. Don't panic when you hear these. Instead, pray. Ask God to help your children be a light in a world, and ask your kids how you can help them do this.

3) Ask your kids or your grandkids what they are already doing to demonstrate God's love for their friends. You might be surprised what you learn. One time when I asked one of my children this, I found out that they had been buying lunch for a kid who couldn't afford it. If your children have Jesus, they are already missionaries—celebrate their work.

4) Examine your own heart for the kind of pride that demands that you defend your stance rather than listen to the other perspective.

5) Do not allow yourself to be offended by ideas. Relationships matter more than being right.

6) Ask God to open your eyes so that you can see where pride is the motivation for being unwilling to consider another's opinion and see another's problems with the same urgency and attention that you see your own.

7) Ask your pastor if you can teach a kids' class. Help them to learn that they are all equally gifted as leaders in God's Kingdom and that God has a place for each one of them.

8) Talk to the youth pastor of your church. Find out how to pray for our young people. Volunteer.

CHAPTER TWELVE

GREED

"As we are set free by that love from
our own pride and fear, our own greed
and arrogance, so we are free in our turn
to be agents of reconciliation and hope,
or healing and love."
~ N.T. Wright

Just like pride keeps us from seeing others' perspectives through the weeds of self-importance, so does greed, because self-importance has bloomed into something that demands repayment.

In recent years, there have been a significant number of scholars who have dedicated their studies to the challenges found in the American Church. Documentaries have been produced, articles written, and social media posts created at an incredible pace. The distressing thing is when I ask other people in the Church if they have read or watched any of these, typically they are not even aware of them.

Part of this is, of course, due to the overabundance of articles that one can now read. But I think part of it is also that we simply do not want to be called into account.

Therefore, we have continued on our merry way, oblivious to the changes that are happening and being talked about in the larger society. This is a problem.

For years, people have talked about greed in the Church. I remember as a kid seeing people roll their eyes at the thought of the Crystal Cathedral while commenting about how many people *that* building could have fed. And while I hesitate to dive too deep into criticism over how any church spends their money—primarily because most churches are not in the category where their ministers are flying in private planes and driving cars that cost more than my annual household income—the topic deserves to be discussed.

The average church size in the United States is easily below one hundred people. For every one mega church with a pastor who walks around with bodyguards, there are countless other churches where the pastor works a second job to make ends meet. Being bi-vocational is typical for ministers, so it is unfair when people from the outside look in and judge the entire Church as greedy based on the celebrities they see on television.

Where the problem comes in is when those small-church, bi-vocational pastors become discontented with their congregations and think that their ministries should look like those big churches and that that if they don't there must be a failure. Needing to appear successful starts with pride, but it rests in greed. We are greedy for recognition, greedy for financial freedom, greedy for the time back that we had to spend working. This is easily spiritualized, too, because our culture tells us that if we are doing things right, we will find success.

But the heavenly economy does not ascribe to the American culture, no matter how much we tell ourselves it does.

SECULAR MEASURES FOR SUCCESS

Second Corinthians 4:16-18: "So we do not lose heart. Even though our outer nature is wasting away, our inner nature is being renewed day by day. For this slight momentary affliction is preparing us for an eternal weight of glory beyond all measure, because we look not at what can be seen but at what cannot be seen; for what can be seen is temporary, but what cannot be seen is eternal" (NRSV).

Recently, I attended a conference in which other members of my denomination were receiving their credentials. It was a celebration, and I struck up a conversation with the man standing next to me. I learned that he was becoming a licensed minister because he had been serving as a youth pastor when the senior pastor at his church decided to leave his position. He had felt God calling him to take the role, and the church voted him in as their lead pastor.

I asked him how his church was doing, and his response was that they started with about thirty people who attended on Sunday mornings and now they were averaging about forty.

I'm not sure what I expected his response to be, but it wasn't a report on numbers. Maybe I thought he would say something about the work they were doing in the community, or how they were reaching out to the schools and teachers, or even that they had had a killer potluck last weekend.

After being in ministry a while and talking to other pastors, I learned that this response—a focus on numbers as an indicator of health—was the typical response.

How did we get here?

Later that evening, I was listening to the keynote speaker, and he made the statement that if you are a pastor, and you are over fifty-five and your church has stopped growing, that maybe it is time for you to move on and give a younger pastor the chance to try to grow the church.

Most of the people in the room applauded, but looking around the room, my heart broke for those small-church pastors who were in their fifties, who served in rural communities, and the pressure they must feel.

And that's when it occurred to me that my dad had also fallen prey to this kind of thinking. I remember him saying that if the church didn't significantly grow by a certain point in his ministry, that he would make plans to retire. I now realize that this numbers-based standard of success is not biblical.

A successful church is a church that makes disciples. A successful church is a church that offers comfort, that stands as a beacon of unity in their communities, that demonstrates that different people from different backgrounds can work together and serve in Jesus's name.

A SUCCESSFUL CHURCH IS A CHURCH THAT MAKES DISCIPLES.

A successful church is one where the pastor shepherds the flock. One where the pastor walks with their congregations as they marry, have children, get new jobs, follow God's calling, and reach out to the community.

A successful pastor is one that inspires others to work for the Kingdom, whether that is going into ministry or bringing Jesus to the workplace.

A successful pastor is not to be worried about numerical growth; a successful pastor is to be concerned with the spiritual growth of those God has placed under his or her care.

A successful pastor can be one who has spent his or her entire life in a small-town church, preaching and loving the flock and the community, and if that church began as a group of thirty people and ended as a group of thirty people, the pastor has served God honorably.

A pastor is a disciple of Jesus who disciples other followers of Christ so that they are encouraged to walk closer to Him.

Part of my current job is to watch over our church plants and to make sure things stay on track between the campuses and the parent church. This has allowed me to see firsthand the pressure that small-church pastors are under to grow into communities that look like the ones that we can see on YouTube and other media.

The most tragic part is that when pastors push for their churches to look like other, more famous, churches, they are slipping into the trap of building a church that takes after *their* vision rather than God's.

Dietrich Bonhoeffer recognized the danger and the tragedy in this over seventy years ago when he said:

> "Every human idealized image that is brought into the Christian community is a hindrance to genuine community and must be broken up so that genuine community can survive. Those who love their dream of a Christian community more than the Christian community itself become destroyers of that Christian community even though their personal intentions may be ever so honest, earnest, and sacrifi-

cial. God hates this wishful dreaming because it makes the dreamer proud and pretentious. Those who dream of this idealized community demand that it be fulfilled by God, by others, and by themselves. They enter the community of Christians with their demands, set up their own law, and judge one another accordingly. They stand adamant, a living reproach to all others in the circle of the community. They act as if they must create the Christian community, as if their visionary ideal binds the people together. Whatever does not go their way, they call a failure. When their idealized image is shattered, they see the community breaking into pieces. So, they first become accusers of other Christians in the community, then accusers of God, and finally the desperate accusers of themselves."

In short, when we approach ministry with our vision of what success should look like, we are doomed to fail by both our standards as well as God's standards.

When people who have been in the Church migrate out of the Church, and when they cite these measures of success as a reason, we must admit that they are seeing something that we might not be seeing, or at least something that we do not want to see.

There are very few reasons for our reluctance except our greed.

We are greedy for success.

As pastors, we want our message to get out to as many people as possible because we know the power inherent in the words of our Lord. But God may have other plans for our ministries.

There is a letter sent to all ministers who receive their credentials through the Assemblies of God. In this letter, they include a prayer from John Wesley that puts into perspective the drive to be successful by any standards other than God's:

> "Lord Jesus, if you will receive me in to your house, if you will own me as your servant, I will not stand upon terms; impose upon me what conditions you please, write down your own articles, command me what you will, put me to anything you see as good; let me come under your roof, let me be your servant...make me what you will, Lord, and set me where you will...I put myself wholly into your hands: put me to what you will, rank me with whom you will; put me to doing, put me to suffering, let me be employed for you, or laid aside for you, exalted for you, or trodden under foot for you; let me be empty, let me have

all things, let me have nothing. I freely and heartily resign all to your pleasure and disposal."

This is a pastor's heart.

When we stray from this truth—the truth that we might never be and should never try to be successful by earthly standards—we begin working in our own power.

The job is too big for that. We, as pastors, as leaders in God's mission, are not enough. We cannot build a church on our vision, and if we do, it is not a church…it is a business that masquerades as a church.

And the people you want in your church—the ones who are steadily growing closer to God, the ones who are learning to die to themselves, the ones who want to be a representative of Jesus here on earth—those ones will see through the façade, and they will leave.

Have we lost people because they see something we do not?

WHAT CAN WE DO?

1) Thank your pastors for their work and for their sacrifices…especially the financial ones. Being satisfied to serve in a community of believers that does not have the monetary resources that the big-

ger churches have means that your pastors are often committing themselves to working multiple jobs for the privilege of fulfilling their call.

2) If you are part of a big church (or any church) volunteer, invite people, and find ways to create community that are based on your shared beliefs. If you are part of a large church because it means that you can belong without serving, then you are there for the wrong reason. Christians serve. It is the hallmark of one who follows Christ.

3) When you look around and see someone missing, take the initiative and call them yourself. Don't wait for church leadership. You are the Church.

4) Protect the Church by caring for people.

CHAPTER THIRTEEN

CELEBRITY CULTURE IN THE CHURCH

This criticism builds off the last one. When we are focused on meeting non-biblical standards of success in our churches, then it is natural that to meet those measures, we are drawn to people who exude success as defined by our culture.

It's ironic, because one of the things that the Church points to as a danger to the Church is the infiltration of the outside culture into the Church. Often, we fail to see it, or at least choose to ignore it, in this regard.

When we talk about the Church succumbing to the forces outside of the Church, even from our own pulpits, we tend to think of the acceptance of sins and worldviews that are outside of what the modernist majority thought for so long to be appropriate. We talk of churches that have decided to loosen their stances on homosexuality or abortion or drinking or whatever hard lines your particular denomination has drawn.

Again, I am not going to debate these issues in these pages. My goal is to simply point out that while we seem to have no problem seeing the things that make us uncomfortable and preaching against those, we often fail to see the other things that are equally, if not more dangerous to the Church body. It's easy to point out the things that we might not struggle with, but when it comes to pride or greed—both sins that dig down to the very heart of the fall of humankind and our continued failure to do what we are called to do (stand as a witness to God's goodness and love)—we willingly remain ignorant.

We don't have to focus on one or the other. If you are reading this, and you are going to ask "what about_____," filling in the blank with an example of what you think is the worst sin, then I am begging you to step away from that defensive stance. We can maintain our beliefs regarding what our denominations call sin while at the same time look honestly at the sins that we have mistakenly come to accept. And by the way, sin is sin.

Those who have chosen to stand outside the fold of the Church are not perfect. We also are not perfect, but we have received grace. Having received grace, we are called to offer grace. Folks now outside the Church may not be correct in everything they say or believe about the Church, they may have made sweeping generalizations based on their personal experience, but they are coming from a place of hurt, so we can at least listen without pointing out the things we do not agree with. We can at least look honestly and assess whether they have a point.

Before I took the position in the Church where I currently serve, I decided I should wander a bit on Sunday mornings and see what some of the other churches in the area were doing. The lead pastor of my church was considering planting new works in the surrounding cities, and I wanted to get a feel for the area and how the local churches were serving their communities.

There were some great moments and some not-so-great moments, but the thing that stood out to me the most was that everyone seemed to be following the same formula: dark rooms, pastors in skinny jeans, worship leaders who looked like they were barely out of high school, well thought out brochures and advertising, Apple computers at the check-in stations, coffee shops, café-height tables, good places for Instagram photos, reminders to like everything on Facebook, invites for small groups that focused on common interests or life stages littered here and there, and a million other details that were somehow all taken out of the same playbook.

There's nothing wrong with any of it—it's supposed to bring people in. Although, I do have to admit, with going to so many churches that were doing all the same thing, it did start to feel a little cult-ish. I could see why some of the people in the #exvangelical movement call evangelicalism a cult. If you are on the outside looking in, the sameness could be overwhelming.

Notwithstanding the strangeness of so many places that seem to have all gone to the Chip and Joanna Gaines school of decorating, the environment is supposed to create welcoming places to talk and areas to find others who share your interests. It's supposed to make people feel safe. It's supposed to be engaging and uplifting and make guests feel like they are at home.

The one thing that was missing were the hosts—the pastors were nowhere to be found.

Now, I know that for pastors it can be difficult to balance those moments right before service when your heart should be in an attitude of prayer whilst navigating a mob of people who want to talk to you. The same can be said for after service when the pastor is understandably exhausted. It isn't easy to be available all the time to everyone who wants a piece of the pastor.

But that's the job.

And that's when I realized what was happening.

If you look at the mega-church pastors on YouTube or any other media, or if you visit one of their massive churches, you will notice that the pastor is not hobnobbing with the people. Rather, the pastor comes out during the last few chords of the worship team's final song, and he or she retreats to the recesses of the stage immediately after the sermon is completed.

Like a rock star.

And then I started looking around again. Skinny jeans, check. Dark sanctuaries, check. Insane stage lighting, check. Advertising, check. Smoke machines…

It occurred to me that maybe the small churches that are stretching their budgets are doing so to look like the big boys. This wouldn't be a problem—if something works to bring people in, why not try it. But the reality that they are copying the mega-church pastors to the point that they are not connecting with the people reveals a deeper truth.

They want to be mega-church pastors, too.

The fact that we are willing to sacrifice relationships in order to look more like the mega churches reveals that our motives are more about looking like worldly success than success as defined by Jesus's example. It would be different if the pastors who are trying to be trendy were really copying the big churches in hopes of reaching more people for Christ. But why would a pastor with 200 people in the seats enter and exit by stage, remaining unavailable to their congregation? It's a question we must ask.

We need to remember the priorities of the first church. We need to remember what is important in our services. In fact, Paul responded to the factions that had developed in the Corinthian church because some were following Paul and others were identifying with Apollos.

In chapter 3 of 1 Corinthians, Paul says: "And so, brothers and sisters, I could not speak to you as spiritual people, but rather as people of the flesh, as infants in Christ. I fed you with milk, not solid food, for you were not ready for solid food. Even now you are still not ready, for you are still of the flesh. For as long as there is jealousy and quarreling among you, are you not of the flesh, and behaving accordingly to human inclinations? For when one says, 'I belong to Paul,' and another 'I belong to Apollos,' are you not merely human?" (verses 1-4, NRSV).

Factions had arisen in the Corinthian church because the congregation was identifying with their leaders rather than the unifying identity of Christ. Therefore, Paul says they are fed milk—because their desire to be known by the person whose teachings they followed revealed their immaturity.

Later in the chapter, Paul goes on to explain why his ministry and Apollos's ministry were different, hoping that the congregation would understand that Paul was the one who "planted the seed" and "Apollos watered" it.

This provides even a greater depth of danger to what we are already seeing: If our desire for success spurs us on to emulate the churches that we define as successful by human standards, this means that our churches are adopting the same practices, teachings, and training. This leaves the question of who is planting and who is watering.

Different Christians perform different tasks for the body. If we are all trying to be the same, there are jobs that are not getting done.

> DIFFERENT CHRISTIANS PERFORM DIFFERENT
> TASKS FOR THE BODY. IF WE ARE ALL TRYING
> TO BE THE SAME, THERE ARE JOBS THAT
> ARE NOT GETTING DONE.

We may be self-correcting in this already.

After the Covid shutdown and the ensuing struggle to get our worlds back up and running, a trend has been emerging. Anecdotally, because I do not think enough time has gone by yet for serious studies to have been completed, it seems like the smaller congregations have been rebounding faster than the larger ones.

This tells us a few things. First, our people are hungry for the family atmosphere of the smaller communities. This shouldn't surprise any of us after the isolation. Second, we've all had to make adjustments in our own personal finances, reprioritizing when necessary. Suddenly, going to a building that costs $10K a month to heat feels opulent and a little out of step with where most people are right now.

Being part of a family doesn't require those things, and home churches and tiny storefront congregations are again sprouting up to meet the needs of the community and to disciple those who are hungry to know more about their Savior.

In seminary, even before the pandemic, I was hearing from more and more pastors about their plan to stay bi-vocational, not expecting ever to be able to support themselves completely from their ministry efforts. This feels hopeful to me. Out of the airless trap of stress as they tried to look successful to draw more people in, and out of the fire of self-doubt when their efforts were not met with earthly success, and out of the ashes of a life of comparison and sameness, ministers are rising up to do God's work because they are called. They are responding to that call like Abraham did—they are demonstrating their love for God despite the personal return. This speaks of a growing maturity. One we may not have noticed that we lacked in some places—but other people did.

WHAT CAN WE DO?

1) If you are in the search for a church home, look deeper than the marketing and hype. Watch to see how the pastor interacts with the congregants. Is he or she genuinely interested in the spiritual growth of the individuals under his or her care? Is discipleship the primary focus of the church?

2) Pray and read the Bible. Nothing protects us more from being misled than those two things.

3) The next time you are asked to promote something

on social media, consider if your promotion changes anything. Our culture has tricked us into feeling like promotion is action. It is not. I would challenge you, for every hashtag campaign you share, do something that takes more effort than moving your thumbs. If you share a post about human trafficking, go to the site and donate $5. If you share a post about your church's event, pick up the phone and personally invite a friend. If you share a quote from the Bible, spend the time to look up the verse and read it in context. The only way we can win the battle against celebrity culture in the church is to do so with authenticity.

CHAPTER FOURTEEN

PROTECTED LEADERS OVER VICTIMS

This is a difficult topic, and one that we do not need to spend much time on because, with the number of people who have come forward, there is no way to argue that this has not happened and that our response as the Church has been insufficient.

While one denomination can point fingers at another, the fact is that in order to protect the Church, the leadership, and the business of doing church, there have been far, far too many abuse victims that have been ignored, maligned, and silenced.

The only way forward with this issue is to apologize and ask for forgiveness both from God and those who have had bad experiences.

For too long we have adopted a stance of protection for the Church as an organization when we should have been protecting those who are the Church.

It's difficult when someone from the outside looking in points to us with censure and they are right.

We have been greedy to keep things going, keep the lights on, keep the majority happy, when there are those amongst us who have suffered unspeakable pain. In the end, we have chosen us over them, our comfort over their healing. In doing so, we have been complicit as the perpetrators have racked up distressingly long lists of victims.

All because we didn't want to deal with it, or we were afraid to deal with it.

The tragedy is that there are so many good churches and good pastors out there—far outnumbering the bad ones. But when faced with a cascade of failures to this extent, all of us have work to do.

That same spirit that made us protect the Church in the first place now calls us to truly protect the Church. Only this time, instead of denial or disregard we do so through collective repentance.

You may balk at the idea, but there is biblical foundation for repentance as a community.

At some level, we are all guilty of perpetuating the culture within the Church that required us not to ask questions or to sit by silently when something seemed off. It is at the very heart of the other issues on the list. We have been complicit because we perpetuated a climate where those who questioned were the dangerous ones. Sadly, we have found out that it is the exact opposite.

Maybe you are thinking that this one is a bit of a stretch. After all, your church might never have experienced anything like this. So, I ask, are there other areas of abuse that you have overlooked because to dive in would have potentially risked the peace in the church? Are there things that have cropped up in the congregation that you might have dealt with differently had that church member not have been a volunteer, or a regular tither?

How have we responded when it came to light that a board member had been verbally abusing his wife for years? Was she counseled to keep the peace? Was she reminded that God hates divorce?

What about the parents whose parenting techniques cause a few raised eyebrows and are the reason behind more than one sleepless night of prayer for the kids' ministries teams?

What else have we remained quiet about?

I am not advocating for a witch hunt of everyone whose family dynamics do not line up with what we think is godly, I'm only saying that we need to be ready and able to ask questions in love and according to the mandates found in Matthew 18.

And if those questions are met with resistance, we need to be prepared to help the victim despite what we see as possible fall-out. People have to matter more than the organization because if we take care of the people, we are taking care of the Church.

> WE NEED TO BE PREPARED TO HELP THE VICTIM DESPITE WHAT WE SEE AS POSSIBLE FALL-OUT. PEOPLE HAVE TO MATTER MORE THAN THE ORGANIZATION.

WHAT CAN WE DO?

1) Do not diminish another's pain. Ever.

2) If you become aware of abuse of any kind, report it. Abuse is not conflict. When there is conflict in the Church, we follow Matthew 18. Abuse is different. We protect those who are in danger.

3) Do not assume that just because someone is from a wealthy or successful family, that allegations of abuse couldn't be true.

4) When you hear someone from outside of the Church talk about abuse in the Church, be ready to tell them what your church has done to help people be safe. Talk about practical things like windows in all doors and children's policies that require more than one adult in every room. Work to change the perception that the Church protects their own and build a reputation for protecting the weakest.

CHAPTER FIFTEEN

IDOLATRY

"Faith is not the clinging to a shrine but
an endless pilgrimage of the heart."
~ Abraham Joshua Heschel

Once pride and greed have a foothold in our churches, the development of idolatry is inevitable because even though we might say that God is the most important person in our lives, the reality at this point is that we are.

If, through pride, we become convinced our habits and practices are sanctioned by God, and this paves the way for our greed to be justified, then it is not much of a leap to wind up in a place where we think the issues and stances important to us are the ones that are primary to God. It is here where we slip into idolatry. It is here where we begin worshiping the things that made us proud and fooled us into thinking we deserve repayment.

The problems listed in the next chapters are those that

are amongst the most often heard from the #exvangelicals or the deconstructors, and they are the ones that have revealed some truths that the Church absolutely does not want to grapple with.

The problems here exist on that line where politics and religion meet.

In the United States, this line is less of a fence and more of an entire pasture where people can graze their whole life, never realizing the danger they are doing to God's Kingdom. You see, while there is a distressing amount of pride and greed embedded in politics, for the Church, idolatry is at the very heart of the matter, because we are idolizing our present situation and struggles over the vision of the future that God has given us.

When we put our issues before God's issues, when we fall into the trap of not being able to separate the two, we are living an idolatrous life.

IGNORING THE VOICES

On top of the pandemic and the political unrest due to the election year, 2020 brought us the horrific reminder of our failure to reconcile the centuries-long problem of racial bias and discrimination, as well as continued to widen the gulf between those who have financial stability and those who struggle with poverty.

As I write this, I am aware that there are those who think racism is alive and well and those who do not agree.

There are those who think that economically challenged people face difficulty only because of their poor choices, and those who think poverty is primarily a societal ill. I am making the choice in these pages not to argue the validity of either side. Instead, I want to remind the Church that when there are those who are in pain, who are scared, and who feel trapped and hopeless by their realities, the Christian response is to help.

It does not matter whether or not you believe a person justified in their fear. If we are following Christ's example, we find a way to ease that fear. If someone is hungry, we find a way to feed them. If someone is hurt, we find a way to heal them.

I am as Caucasian as people can get. The farthest south my DNA hails from is France. As such, I have no right to speak one way or another about the challenges that people of color face in the United States. I also grew up on the lower end of middle class, and I haven't had to go to bed hungry or without heat, so I have very little to draw on personally when speaking of poverty.

I can, however, speak from my limited experiences living in a predominantly poor neighborhood and talk about my observations.

About eight years ago, I, my husband, and our three youngest children decided to move next door to a non-profit that served an impoverished area with a health clinic, food pantry, and other services. We worked at that mission for about a year, but one night stands out as particularly memorable.

In our apartment complex, we were in the minority not only because of our ethnicity, but because of our economic position. We didn't have a lot, but still much more in comparison to others who shared our building.

This area of Milwaukee, WI was (and remains) one of the poorest zip codes in the nation. Densely populated and distressingly segregated, the crime rate was astronomical, drug use was rampant, single-parent families were the norm, and few people had access to vehicles. Even fewer had consistent access to health care and emergency economic resources. It was not uncommon for us to scramble to find a coat for a child who was missing school because it was too cold to walk and they had no winter gear.

One evening, my husband was late coming home from work. I had just picked up the kids from school. (They were enrolled in a private school that did not suffer from a 60% graduation rate—yet another privilege we had in comparison to our neighbors.) We had barely dropped our bags at the door after climbing ten flights of stairs because the elevator was out of order…again. We were tired, hungry, crabby, cold, and ready to settle in for an evening of homework and dinner.

That's when our youngest child, who was about seven at the time, informed me that she needed poster board for a school project the next day.

I wanted to cry. I had just fought my way through forty-five minutes of traffic on slush-covered winter roads, dragged three kids through an icy parking lot, only to find the elevator broken.

I sent the offending child my best mom look, bundled them all back up, and headed back down to the car so that we could go find poster board.

In the section of the city where we lived, there were no convenient stores. Not even grocery stores. In fact, it's what they call a food desert—a place in the heart of the city where there are only fast-food options and shady corner marts that sell alcohol, lottery tickets, tobacco, and junk food. So, we had to drive miles away to one of the worst Walmarts I have ever been in. We all piled out of the car, grabbed a cart, trudged through the slush (it was snowing again by now), and into the store. Only to find that they were out of poster board.

Back in the car we went and on to the next Walmart another five miles away.

I won't continue torturing you with the mundane details of the rest of the trip, but when we finally returned home at nearly 8:30 p.m., we were done. I have no idea if everyone's homework got finished that night; I know the teachers' letters home went unread, and I think dinner ended up being mac and cheese.

I tucked the kids in much later than they should have

been, and I sat down on the couch, stunned into a stupor by the intensity of our evening.

That's when it hit me.

If I had been a typical mother in our apartment building, I would have been working two jobs for minimum wage, often sixty or more hours per week. I would have come home late at night to kids who would have finished their day at a failing school and come home to a house with no parents. If my youngest child needed something from the store, my first decision that night would have been if I should even try to get through the slush and cold and make it to a store to get the poster board.

I would have had to know the bus schedule and be prepared to spend hours and transfers just to get to where I needed to go. I would also have to decide whether to leave my children warm, hopefully safe, but unattended at home while I tried to find the school supplies, or I would have had to make the decision to take them out in the cold and damp with me. I would have had to pay bus fare for me and my kids. I would have had to manage all this for two stores.

I would have had to get that poster board back without water damage from snow or creases from a rogue gust of wind. I would have had to try to figure out what to feed them, and if I should feed them before or after we left—which would depend on the bus schedule.

And that's just the start of the list.

What I learned that day was that it would take an incredible person to manage all of that just so their child would have poster board and the best chance at a good day at school the next day.

So, when I hear people say that if those in poverty really wanted to get out, they could, I have to disagree. You see, I'm not sure if my situation were the same as most of the people who lived in the same apartment complex as me, if I would have been a tenacious enough mother to help my children escape the trap of poverty. Even with all my privileges, I was tired and close to tears just from the stresses brought on by the environment.

The problem with inequality and injustice is that those of us who have even limited power to change things often refuse to trade in enough of our assumptions to meet the problems with empathy. We are proud of what we have accomplished—never mind that our set of experiences is vastly different from the other person's—we want what is our due and have grown used to getting our way, and we become convinced that our way of life, our decisions, and our habits are the best ones possible.

The problem is that instead of serving others like we are required to as Christians, we justify our inaction by vilifying those who are not living like we think they should.

Idolatry is not just worshiping other gods. Anything that we allow to keep us from God is also an idol. And if our ideas about the character or culture of another person are what keep us from serving others, then our ideas are our idols. They keep us from growing closer to Christ.

> IF OUR IDEAS ABOUT THE CHARACTER OR CULTURE OF ANOTHER PERSON ARE WHAT KEEP US FROM SERVING OTHERS, THEN OUR IDEAS ARE OUR IDOLS.

Those who have left the Church see this. They see that we are more dedicated to our ideas than we are to the ideas of Christ. We can't ignore this.

WHAT CAN WE DO?

1) Purposely read reports and watch videos that you think will disagree with your point of view. Do this with the goal of understanding why the person in the report thinks differently than you do. Fight the urge to argue about it, simply see what you can learn.

2) Read the Gospels. Meditate on the accounts of Jesus and His interactions with people.

3) Read or listen to stories written by people who do not look like you.

4) Serve in soup kitchens. Serve the homeless. If Jesus were walking the earth right now, I don't think the first place He would visit would be a gorgeous mega church. Spend time where Jesus would spend time.

CHAPTER SIXTEEN

CHRISTIAN NATIONALISM

From a pastor's perspective, besides the loss of life due to Covid, the fractures in the Church that began in 2020 were one of the most heartbreaking things I have ever witnessed.

It was a slow death, with people every day making tiny decisions to choose their perspectives over the health of the body of believers.

The isolation and illness brought a powerlessness than none of us were prepared for, and when we lack power, we get defensive and lash out.

Add to that the divided political climate, where people are now voting against what they don't believe rather than for what they do believe, and the months of 2020 were a tinderbox of unhealthy emotion exasperated by the need to hold on to power and force others to hear us.

One of the most often quoted reasons people give for leaving the Church is the political climate that exists within the Church. This is tragic.

When we come to know Christ, all our other identities fade in the shadow of our new purpose—to spread hope and love and justice and freedom in the message of the gospel. If we are Christians, the other things do not matter because our unity in mission is what draws people to the Church.

> WHEN WE COME TO KNOW CHRIST,
> ALL OUR OTHER IDENTITIES FADE
> IN THE SHADOW OF OUR NEW PURPOSE.

We have failed in this.

Not only were we disunified, but we were downright angry with those who didn't agree with us.

And you might think that your points of view are the only valid ones and that you are right in all your stances. I'm here to tell you that if you gave any of those points of view priority over your relationships with those in the body of Christ and thereby hurt your witness, you were wrong.

The truth is your dedication to your mission as a Christian is more important than your political party.

Your dedication to your mission as a Christian is more important than your opinion on masks or vaccines or who you voted for.

Your dedication to your mission as a Christian is more important than being right.

During the pandemic, pastors had to walk the line between those who thought wearing masks meant that people lacked faith and those who thought that not wearing masks meant people lacked love. Both sides supported their points of view with Bible verses, and pastors were in the line of fire.

In our church, we lost some people because they thought we were too willing to require masks and others because they thought that we were not strict enough. But the real reason we lost people is because they lacked the understanding of what Christian community is supposed to be and lacked the spiritual maturity to separate their politics from their responsibilities as disciples of Jesus.

As pastors, we can't escape that this is partly our fault. We assumed our congregations were more grounded in Christian principles than they were. Maybe that was a little pride or arrogance on our part—we thought we had done a better job. Maybe it was because we have had so many decades of relative peace within our churches, and we were lulled into thinking that the peace had something to do with the way we ran our organizations. Or maybe there is an upheaval whenever adversity is experienced.

Whatever the reason, we were not as prepared as we thought we were.

The outside world is pointing in, and one of the most common indictments is about what they call the rise of Christian nationalism.

When I talk to people in the Church, they really have no idea what this means, so to make sure we are all on the same page, I will describe it.

Christian nationalism is the idea that the world outside should reflect Christian ideals, and in America, that Christians have a right to expect this because of what they see as a heritage of Christian tradition.

The problem is that we live in a post-Christian society. Why in the world would people who are not Christians live by Christian standards?

Not to mention that even within Christian communities, what constitutes Christian standards can vary from one congregation to another. This means that not only do we try to impose our standards on those who have no reason to follow our standards, but also, we do so with irregularity and with conflicting requirements.

There is only one way to resolve this. We have to behave like Christians who happen to be American, not Americans who happen to be Christians.

THERE IS ONLY ONE WAY TO RESOLVE THIS.
WE HAVE TO BEHAVE LIKE CHRISTIANS
WHO HAPPEN TO BE AMERICAN,
NOT AMERICANS WHO HAPPEN
TO BE CHRISTIANS.

Romans 12:9-21 reminds us of the marks of a true Christian:

> "Let love be genuine; hate what is evil, hold fast to what is good; love one another with mutual affection; outdo one another in showing honor. Do not lag in zeal, be ardent in spirit, serve the Lord. Rejoice in hope, be patient in suffering, persevere in prayer. Contribute to the needs of the saints; extend hospitality to strangers. Bless those who persecute you; bless and do not curse them. Rejoice with those who rejoice, weep with those who weep. Live in harmony with one another; do not be haughty, but associate with the lowly; do not claim to be wiser than you are. Do not repay anyone evil for evil, but take thought for what is noble in the sight of all. If it is possible, so far as it depends on you, live peaceably with all. Beloved, never avenge yourselves, but leave room for the wrath of God; for it is written, 'Vengeance is mine, I will repay, says the Lord.' No, 'if your enemies are hungry, feed them; if they are thirsty, give them something to drink; for by doing this you will heap burning coals on their heads.'

Do not be overcome by evil, but overcome evil with good" (NRSV).

No part of those verses that define what a true Christian is says anything about asserting our will on those who do not believe. Quite the opposite; these verses remind us that it is our sacrifice that draws others in. In these verses, God does not demand that we defend our beliefs, God demands that we live them.

It is a high call.

WHAT CAN WE DO?

1) Pray for our nation. Pray for our leaders.

2) Pray that the people of God's Church will remember that their biggest witness is not their words, but their actions.

3) When you are about to argue about politics, pause for a minute and ask yourself if it hurts or helps your witness.

4) Be humble and accept that you do not have all the answers.

5) Learn to be comfortable with choosing to preserve relationships rather than being right.

CHAPTER SEVENTEEN

RADICAL HUMILITY

In the Bible, we are reminded over and over again that we are to be humble, radically humble. We are to live Jesus's example, and by doing so, we are to change the world.

We will not change the world through our pride, through our greed, or through making idols of our own ideals. We will not change the world by demanding that those outside the Church conform to the ways of the Church. It was always understood that Christians would stand out, be different, and live like we know that "our citizenship is in heaven" (Philippians 3:20).

In our attempt to be set apart, though, we somehow shifted the burden of that decision from ours to theirs, expecting others to accept that we are set apart, and that is not in the Bible. In doing so, we argue, we demand, we move into positions of power, we bring power structures into the Church that were never part of Christ's Church, and we end up looking exactly like the outside world.

This is why those who have left are so vocal. They can see what we cannot. They see that the Church has become like the world.

> IN OUR ATTEMPT TO BE SET APART, WE SOMEHOW SHIFTED THE BURDEN OF THAT DECISION FROM OURS TO THEIRS, EXPECTING OTHERS TO ACCEPT THAT WE ARE SET APART.

Part of maturity is understanding that our definitions change, grow, and sometimes expand. When I used to hear of people talking about the Church becoming like the world, I thought in terms of obvious sins, of accepting things within the body of believers that would not bring glory to God. As I've grown, though, I think that while this can be part of it, it does not need to be our main concern.

Our main concern should be us. Individually. Are we reflecting the image of God to each other and to the outside world?

If we all do this, then those big sins—the pet sins—the ones that first come to mind when we hear the word "sin," will be revealed as the dust on the table—because there is so much more underneath.

Pride runs deep, so does greed and idolatry.

And humility is difficult to come by.

A couple of years ago, I wanted to do a teaching on

humility. The concept intrigued me because the Bible talks about it all the time, and I think most of us, myself included, tend to think that if we aren't proclaiming from the mountaintops how awesome we are, then we have a good handle on humility.

I turned to the Internet to look for teachings on humility, and I stumbled across Mother Teresa's suggestions for how to practice humility. This changed everything for me. Here is what she said:

1) Speak as little as possible about yourself.

2) Keep busy with your own affairs and not those of others.

3) Avoid curiosity.

4) Do not interfere in the affairs of others.

5) Accept small irritations with good humor.

6) Do not dwell on the faults of others.

7) Accept censures even if unmerited.

8) Give in to the will of others.

9) Accept insults and injuries.

10) Accept contempt, being forgotten and disregarded.

11) Be courteous and delicate even when provoked by someone.

12) Do not seek to be admired and loved.

13) Do not protect yourself behind your own dignity.

14) Give in, in discussions, even when you are right.

15) Choose always the more difficult task.

Can you imagine how the mission of the Church would change if we would follow this path to humility? Can you picture how different our communities would look if we followed the path of humility that Christ followed all the way to the cross?

If we were as tenacious about emulating Jesus's humility, the Church would not be in a place where we are arguing about where we draw the line between literal and figurative. We would not be obsessed with who could or could not pastor a flock. Or worried about numbers and success by the outside world's standards. We would be protecting the weakest and keeping our minds on our mission rather than allowing ourselves to be distracted by things we cannot control.

Imagine what we could do if we held on to our humility with the same tenacity with which we grasp our pride.

THE GIFT OF MATURITY

Some time ago the WWJD (What Would Jesus Do) movement hit the churches with a revolutionizing force. People wore WWJD bracelets and T-shirts. Youth groups talked about it. Christians tried to live by it. Bible studies were written about it. Even though it has been a couple of decades, people still use the WWJD phrase when faced with an unexpected situation.

Despite the hype and the popularity, looking back, it generally left the Church unchanged, and I wonder if we would not have been better off asking What Would Jesus Do In Me?

While I do not want to diminish the importance of our actions toward others, nor our dedication to holy living, the question of what Jesus would do focuses our attention on how we should interact with those we talk to and live with and do business with every day. It is a worthy focus, but one that might get our priorities a bit out of order.

Bonhoeffer, in his work *Ethics*, reminds us that: "Formation only occurs by being drawn into the form of Jesus Christ, by being conformed to the unique form of the one who became human, was crucified, and is risen. This does not happen as we strive 'to become like Jesus,' as we customarily say, but as the form of Jesus Christ himself so works on us that it molds us, conforming our form to Christ's own."

Charles Spurgeon reminds us that: "One of these days you who are now a 'babe' in Christ shall be a 'father' in the church. Hope for this great thing; but hope for it as a gift of grace, and not as the wages of work, or as the product of your own energy."

If we ask what Jesus would do, then we can get caught

up with trying to instigate change in the world around us in our own power rather than seeking Jesus for the kind of transformation that guides our actions. The question makes an easy path between where we stand and where we want to be, with our actions being the driving force for change. But if we add the "In Me" after that question, it reorients the focus on how Jesus wants to change me to make me a more effective witness to those in my life.

The changes we make happen through our actions will never be as powerful of a witness for Christ as the change He makes happen in us, and eventually through us.

> THE CHANGES WE MAKE HAPPEN THROUGH OUR ACTIONS WILL NEVER BE AS POWERFUL A WITNESS FOR CHRIST AS THE CHANGE HE MAKES HAPPEN IN US, AND EVENTUALLY THROUGH US.

This seems to be the crux of the problems that those who are on the outside looking in now see. Whether or not they have been part of the Church, whether they still love Jesus, whether or not they miss the fellowship or feel freed by the lack of it, the problems that they have listed about the Church all spin around the fact that, as the Church, it seems we have been louder about what we do and what we think and feel than we have about how God is changing us personally.

Christian maturity is a gift. It is not earned after years of doing the right thing. It is not won by putting our faith in the right political party. It is not attained by convincing people that we are right and they are wrong. Spiritual maturity only happens as we gradually accept that we are bearers of God's image, and as such, we are to reflect God's goodness to the world.

Nothing we can do is a stronger witness than the goodness of God.

Being right is not a more convincing example of God's love than grace.

Appearing successful is not more inspiring than living in God's hope.

Denying failure does not make the Church more attractive than living as God asks the Church to live.

We are human. We are flawed. Our love is imperfect, and our sense of justice is wrapped up in our tendency to put ourselves above others. So instead of demanding what we think is right, we should rely on living out the fruits of the Spirit that God has asked us to live.

We demonstrate "love, joy, peace, patience, kindness, generosity, faithfulness, gentleness, and self-control. There is no law against such things" (Galatians 5:22-23, NRSV).

If we think that we can be the final say in matters of justice we will fail because we are not capable of perfect justice, so instead we show love and compassion.

If we try to force others to do what is right in our eyes,

they will not understand, so instead we need to be patient and pray for them.

If we try to convince the people outside of the Church that the Church is the way to health and prosperity, we are lying and those outside of the Church know it. Following Jesus is difficult, it is a path that makes no sense until someone has had an encounter with God. Therefore, we try to be conformed into the image of Christ, and again, we pray for them.

You see, the only change that has keeping power is the change that takes place inside of us. We can't force it on anyone else, and when we try to, they leave, and point back at us with the revelation that we are not living out God's plan. Because God's plan is to change the world one person at a time—starting with us.

What would Jesus do in me?

CHAPTER EIGHTEEN

A NEW START FROM AN OLD EXAMPLE

There is no place in the Bible that gives us a picture of the Church quite like the book of Revelation. It is here where the full story comes into focus, where humanity's choice to define good and evil for themselves comes full circle and God's justice is restored. Revelation is also where we are given a clear picture of the state of the Church when Revelation was written as well as a warning to the future Church.

Just like now, each community had its strengths and weaknesses, and because sin is sin, and people are people, they are remarkably like those we have been discussing in this book.

John is named as the writer of the book, and he begins by describing Jesus as He instructs John to send the letter to the seven churches that he later lists. It is interesting that when giving him direction, the words attributed to Christ are: "'Do not be afraid; I am the first and the last, and the living one. I was dead, and see, I am alive forever and ever; and I have the keys of Death and of Hades. Now write what you have seen, what is, and what is to take place after this'" (Revelation 1:17-19, NRSV).

I find these words comforting. Even in all the unrest, war, and heartbreak that the world has known and will know, Jesus holds the keys, Jesus knows our weaknesses, and Jesus has given instructions that are true for the Church at the time John wrote Revelation as well as now and the time to come. No matter what mistakes we make, no matter where we are strong as the Church or where we are weak, we have these words to reorient ourselves so that we are back in line to do what God asks us to do until the time that all of creation is redeemed. Until we exist in the goodness of God, and until God is once again our source of justice.

If we look at each of these churches, we can see the similarities to where we are today. We can see our mistakes, we can see where our culture has seeped into our practices and our habits, and where we have to take a step back.

We can see how the words of those who have left the Church ring with an ancient familiarity.

EPHESUS

The church of Ephesus was a responsible congregation. They were able to weed out false teachers. They kept the integrity of the teachings, and they didn't "tolerate evildoers"

(Revelation 2:2). They endured and did the right things. But Christ points out: "'You have abandoned the love you had at first'" (Revelation 2:4, NRSV). The Church at Ephesus knew how to be a church, but John's words are a reminder that a church that stays true to doctrine and law and sacrifices love is just as wrong as a church that demonstrates love and ignores truth. The Church of Christ must do both.

When people from outside our churches point out that the Church ignores the voices of the oppressed and chooses instead to point out the sins that the Church deems are the foundation of that oppression, we are seeing this mistake at work. We are seeing how dangerous it is to our witness when we favor law over love.

SMYRNA

Smyrna was the second church that earned Christ's attention, and while there is no censure for this congregation, there is a warning. This congregation lived in a place that was hostile to Christians, with a large community that brought unwanted attention from Rome.

To the Christians in Smyrna, Christ said: "'I know your affliction and your poverty, even though you are rich,'" pointing out the truth that, for the Christian, the lack of material wealth does not translate to a lack of spiritual wealth (Revelation 2:9, NRSV). This community would face persecution and want, but the truth is that persecution and want hold no power over the Church because we are to find our value in other ways.

When those outside of our congregations point out that we spend time emulating the success that we see outside of the Church, we should remember the church in Smyrna that Jesus commended for their sacrifice of material wealth and physical safety.

PERGAMUM

The third church that John writes about is Pergamum. The city where this church existed was filled with those who followed pagan gods and practiced the rituals associated with those gods. Christ says: "'I know where you are living, where Satan's throne is'" (Revelation 2:13, NRSV). Unfortunately, some of the pagan practices had seeped into this church.

John's words plainly point out what needs to be done when the Church conforms to pagan behaviors. "'Repent then.... Let anyone who has an ear listen to what the Spirit is saying to the churches'" (Revelation 2:16-17, NRSV).

When we embrace superstition and build our identity on those beliefs rather than on the truth of God's Word, we are to repent. When we rewrite what the Church should look like and hold an expectation of earthly success rather than one of suffering, we are to repent. God's Church is to be built on the Good News and it is to stay true to it. Becoming distracted by our pet issues and superstitions or adopting the values of the outside community contaminates the message that we send out. Instead of teaching the gospel, we end up preaching the gospel according to us.

Verse seventeen continues to point out the reality of this trap where outside values seep into the Church. You see, we will not recognize this unless we are in communion with the Holy Spirit. Our flesh wants to be successful. Because of this, we are easily deceived into thinking that if we are doing things right, we will find success. This is not the truth. Sometimes we will walk in earthly success, sometimes we will not, but our prosperity is not linked to the depth of our faith. Very faithful people die as martyrs, and very deceitful leaders in the Church drive expensive cars and live in mansions.

When those who have left our congregations point out that the Church does not feel genuine, and that the same drive for success exists inside as well as outside of the Church, they are echoing a problem that is not new. While changing our practices and motivations based on what people outside of the Church are saying seems like the same problem, if what they are saying links all the way back to the churches written about in the book of Revelation, then we should be listening.

THYATIRA

Christ praised the church at Thyatira for its "'works—love, faith, service, and patient endurance'" (Revelation

2:19, NRSV). This congregation had a problem, though. It had allowed a false prophet into its midst and people were being led into sin. John's words reveal that she refused to repent, but the door stayed open for those in the Church to repent.

This church is a strong reminder that we are all responsible for who we follow, what we accept, and how we allow our leaders to change us. These verses carry the reminder that blindly following is dangerous and that in the end, if we do choose to follow someone simply because they have authority, and if we choose to adopt false teachings and doctrines, we are ultimately the ones who will either be rewarded or punished by our choices.

We must ask questions. We must examine motives. We must pray for discernment. Blindly following does not make us good Christians. Blindly following puts us and the body of Christ in danger.

SARDIS

The message to Sardis begins with these words: "'I know your works; you have a name of being alive, but you are dead'" (Revelation 3:1, NRSV).

I am not sure if there is any censure of a church that can be sadder than this. That Christ knows the church by what they do but recognizes that they are spiritually dead should be a warning to us all. Our actions are an expression of our relationship with God. But our actions do not create that relationship.

Again, this is the infiltration of the outside culture into the Church. Action is valuable. It is necessary. But in God's Kingdom, relationship comes first.

AGAIN, THIS IS THE INFILTRATION OF THE OUTSIDE CULTURE INTO THE CHURCH. ACTION IS VALUABLE. IT IS NECESSARY. BUT IN GOD'S KINGDOM, RELATIONSHIP COMES FIRST.

In the Church, we do things for the outside community and for our church families because it is who we are. The action does not define who we are; our relationship with Jesus inspires the action. When churches push action before discipleship, they are disordered.

This links to the greed-driven push to appear successful. If we are doing good things, people get excited for a short time, and they want to be part of what is going on. Eventually, however, they grow weary of doing, and whatever growth or other marker that the Church was using to determine success begins to fade. Unless, of course, there is a constant feed of distraction to bring in new people. This creates a vicious cycle and churches with tons of visitors but few followers of Christ.

When people do things as a natural expression of the

work God is doing in them, though, true disciples are being made. This may or may not translate to numerical growth for the church they belong to, but it does guarantee that the church is growing spiritually and the gospel is being shared.

The Church hears all the time from those who have left that the people in the Church are not genuine. This is one of the reasons. Even people who are not living for God can tell when those who claim to be living for God are living for their own goals.

PHILADELPHIA

Philadelphia gives us hope. Like Sardis, Christ says, "'I know your works'" (Revelation 3:8), but unlike Sardis, the works of this church find favor. Christ continues: "'I know that you have but little power, and yet you have kept my word and have not denied my name'" (3:8, NRSV). If we needed any reminder that God does not value power the way our culture does, this is it.

The church in Philadelphia, because of their "patient endurance" (3:10) will be kept from the trials that the other churches have faced. Not because they are strong. Not because they are successful, not because of any of the things we tend to value. It is their "patient endurance."

LAODICEA

The last church mentioned in Revelation is the church at Laodicea.

Laodicea is a church that existed in an area that made it easy for their church members to financially prosper, but Jesus reminds them that although they might be wealthy and successful, they are "wretched, pitiable, poor, blind, and naked" because they have become complacent in their faith. The church members have forgotten that they need God, that their successful existence is only a breath of forever, and the moments they are rich on earth are being purchased with an eternity of despair.

The most famous part of these verses is when Christ tells the church not to be lukewarm. This is interesting, because it is often taught as if being lukewarm is a measure of our faith. But here, the mention of lukewarm water is closely linked to the geography of Laodicea.

Laodicea did not have a good source of water on its own, but north of Laodicea was Hierapolis which was known for their hot springs; and south of Laodicea was Colossae, which was known for its clean, cold springs. Laodiceans would have to get water from one of these two places, but by the time it got back to Laodicea, it was lukewarm and not useful for drinking or washing.

This metaphor is perfect for the state that the church was in. It was prosperous, wealthy, and successful by the world's standards, but inside, it was useless. The story of this church is a warning to all churches, and particularly applicable to our churches today. Wealth and success corrupt churches just like they corrupt other organizations, and when the Church adopts secular measures for success, we don't even see it coming.

When the Church does not come to the assistance of those who are hurting, when the Church is more concerned with numbers than they are with spiritual growth, the Church ceases to be the Church. When the Church seeks to gain power, when the Church embraces identities other than the one that unites us all, the Church ceases to be the Church. It is no wonder why, when faced with the difficulties of these past few years, the Church has floundered.

It is easy to be a Christian when things are easy, and it is easy to trick ourselves into thinking that we are Christians when things are going well. Eventually, though, the lack of discipleship, the lack of spiritual maturity, the lack of relationship with Jesus will surface, and what is revealed is a Church that is not as strong as it thought it was and as useless to the Kingdom as lukewarm water.

THE LACK OF DISCIPLESHIP, THE LACK OF SPIRITUAL MATURITY, THE LACK OF RELATIONSHIP WITH JESUS WILL SURFACE, AND WHAT IS REVEALED IS A CHURCH THAT IS NOT AS STRONG AS IT THOUGHT IT WAS.

THE OPPORTUNITY

Christ's words to the church at Laodicea end with the famous passage: "'Listen! I am standing at the door, knocking; if you hear my voice and open the door, I will come in to you and eat with you, and you with me'" (Revelation 3:20, NRSV). We often hear these words in sermons that call on new converts to repent. But this verse is speaking to the believers in Laodicea who are blinded by their prosperity. Jesus is asking those of us in the Church to hear His voice, to recognize it, and to once again invite Him in to eat and be a part of our fellowships.

Will we continue to think of these words as a message to those who do not know Jesus, or will we open the door to our hearts, the one Jesus continually knocks at, and listen to what He is trying to tell us? Will we see our own pride, or own greed, and our own idolatry, or will we continue convincing ourselves that Jesus is sitting at our tables, when we have left Him at the door?

CHAPTER NINETEEN

"To clasp the hands in prayer is the
beginning of an uprising against the
disorder of the world."
~ Karl Barth

As Christians, when we look at the chaos and destruction around us, both in individual lives as well as our communities, the temptation is to treat the situation and even the people at the center of the situation as if they were problems and we have the power to fix them.

There is solid reasoning for this: we know the answer. We know that Jesus's example of peace and harmony and patience, that His love and His sacrifice, makes a way for all of us to live in harmony and gives us hope for a future of perfect justice, where no one is lost and where suffering is eradicated.

The drive to force others to live the way we think is right, to accept the truths we accept, and to allow the principles we live by to also rule their lives comes from a good place, but it is a misplaced reflection of our desires rather than God's.

In Luke chapter 4, Jesus faces temptation in the desert. What is revealed in this interaction with the Devil is more than simply that Jesus will refuse to do what the evil one commands; rather, it demonstrates the kind of king that Jesus will be.

Verses 1-13 read as follows:

> "Jesus, full of the Holy Spirit, returned from the Jordan and was led by the Spirit in the wilderness, where for forty days he was tempted by the devil. He ate nothing at all during those days, and when they were over, he was famished. The devil said to him, 'If you are the Son of God, command this stone to become a loaf of bread.' Jesus answered him, 'It is written, "One does not live by bread alone."' Then the devil led him up and showed him in an instant all the kingdoms of the world. And the devil said to him, 'To you I will give their glory and all this authority; for it has been given over to me, and I give it to anyone I please. If you, then, will worship me, it will all be yours.' Jesus answered him, 'It is written, "Worship the Lord your God, and serve only him."' Then the devil took him to Je-

rusalem, and placed him on the pinnacle of the temple, saying to him, 'If you are the Son of God, throw yourself down from here, for it is written, "He will command his angels concerning you, to protect you," and "On their hands they will bear you up, so that you will not dash your foot against a stone."' Jesus answered him, 'It is said, "Do not put the Lord your God to the test."' When the devil had finished every test, he departed from him until an opportune time" (NRSV).

BREAD

It is notable that first, the passage tells us that Jesus was "famished." Facing the kind of hunger that Jesus faced meant that He was tired, He probably was in some pain after not eating for forty days, and He was likely physically weak, had a headache, and was more than ready to get home, eat, and take a bath and a nap.

It is in this weakness that He is approached by Satan. It is when He could become easily frustrated that He is faced with the kinds of deep questions that will reveal what His ministry would look like and how His Kingdom would be ruled.

Satan's first temptation is to remind Jesus that He can use His power to turn the stones into bread so that He could eat and not be hungry. Jesus's response is to point out that bread is not the only thing that matters. Earlier in the Bible, we link this temptation to the account in Deuteronomy when the Israelites, recently freed from slavery, failed to understand that God would be their provider in the desert. Later, we will call Jesus the bread of life, but it is here, in these early chapters of Luke, where we understand that Jesus is the kind of king who is offering a way of life that surpasses what we expect from any human king.

As humans, with our bodies that experience pain and hunger and discomfort, it's tempting to follow anyone who will physically feed us, anyone who will solve the problem of a daily task to keep our bodies fueled and running. A king who gives free bread is a king who will always have a following.

Jesus reveals here that He doesn't want us to follow Him for what we can get from Him or for the simple problems He can solve. Instead, Jesus wants to change our path for eternity. He wants to shape us into people who are future-minded. He wants us to be people who can rightly place this world and the trials of this world into the landscape of forever and understand that if we follow God's path of restoration, bypassing the temptation to latch onto the leadership of anyone who will give us something physical in return, then we can find a glimpse of what it must have been before the fall of humankind. The creation account reminds us that Adam and Eve walked with God and communed with God and lived in relationship with the God who not only could meet their physical needs, but also called them to the deeper satisfaction of a life lived in God's complete justice.

Like Jesus, we have to be strong to grasp this truth and hold on to it while the world clamors for daily bread rather than the bread of life. Through the Holy Spirit, our eyes have been opened to catch a glimpse of the perfect that is to come, but we must understand that this is a revelation, not something learned or proved, and we can't reduce the gospel to something that is easily digestible and hope that the complexities will remain.

We can't simply solve people's problems and hope that Jesus's message of surpassing the troubles of this world will still shine through. The gimmicks and the games we develop in hopes of bringing people into the Kingdom will do the exact opposite. They will create a god for them that is only useful for what they can get now. And as soon as the Church fails to provide whatever the new "believer" thinks it should provide, or as soon as the Church becomes less useful in their everyday scrape to get by, they will fade away from the fellowship, because they had come to the Church for the wrong reason. They were not building a relationship with Christ, instead they were fed a cheap kind of gospel that requires nothing from them but to take.

Relationships are not based on what we can get, they are based on what we will give.

> RELATIONSHIPS ARE NOT BASED
> ON WHAT WE CAN GET, THEY ARE BASED
> ON WHAT WE WILL GIVE.

When Jesus rejects the temptation to reduce His rule to one of simply a provider, He is calling us all to be willing to follow a king who does more than manipulates humanity with material goods. And He is calling the Church to recognize that that kind of leadership is not leadership. It doesn't offer justice; it works in the realm of our pride and greed and vanity, and it does not call us to be better people. It requires nothing from us except that we blindly follow whoever offers us the best bread that wheat can make.

We have to ask ourselves, as the Church—as those who represent Christ on earth—in our attempt to grow our numbers, are we falling to the temptation to try to make things so simple for people that we dumb down the gospel to the point that it is no longer the gospel? Have we turned church into a place where people can go to be entertained, to feel like they belong, to get the occasional freebie, to win a prize, and to spend time with friends instead of the place where people go to grow closer to God?

I am not saying that being in church can't be fun. And I am not saying that the Church should not be serving the community in tangible ways, I am just asking us to evaluate if the way we are instituting these practices is hiding the truth that a life spent following Christ is not going to be an easy life.

Jesus never hid the fact that His decision to be the kind of King we needed instead of the kind of king we wanted would lead to suffering. Once Jesus ascended to heaven, the disciples never worked to spread the gospel with promises of a good life and free loot. Instead, the gospel spread on its true message—life is hard, but you are not alone, and we the Church, are here to support each other as we tell others that life is not just about what kind of bread we can get our hands on to survive. There is more. So much more. There is an eternal hope that we share, and when things get difficult, we are here to remind you that you are loved and seen by the Creator of the universe.

POWER

The second temptation called Jesus, in an instant, to "look at all the kingdoms of the world" and required that He make the decision to keep His allegiance to God and allow the kingdoms of the world to continue to be led as they were while rejecting the offer from Satan to rule immediately.

This must have been excruciating. Jesus was given a vision of all the kingdoms of the world. He would have been able to see the injustice, the failure of leadership, the pride, greed, idolatry, the suffering, and He would have known, in that moment, that He could reign as king and fix all those things.

Satan didn't say that Jesus had to be an evil king. Jesus could have reigned as a just king, Jesus could have righted the wrongs and helped the nations become better. Jesus could have been the king that everyone wanted. But He would have still been working with the dead-end power structure created by humanity and led by Satan.

Instead, Jesus reinforces His dedication to God by quoting the Scripture from Exodus that reminds us to worship only God.

He knew that who we worship is closely linked to how we rule.

When those outside the Church question whether the Church has made idols of humanity's chosen rulers, the question deserves to be considered. When they point out the Church's focus on the outcomes of elections and they bestow their trust and allegiance on the candidate of their choice—hoping that doing so empowers the Church—they are pointing out a temptation to drag the Church into idolatry.

No human can empower the Church, because as soon as we look to a human or a government or any other source other than God to lead us, we are disordered.

It doesn't matter what side of the aisle you hail from, for the Church to seek political power is wrong. Only corruption can result from placing our hope in anything other than God's vision for the future.

The tragedy is that those in the Church often fail to see this. They become caught up in their causes and think that if they can get people to agree with them, then their shared cause will make the Church stronger.

But the Church is only stronger when we draw closer to Christ. The Church is only stronger when relationships are stronger, and dividing along political lines or social issues weakens us no matter how correct we think our stance is.

It might feel like victory when everyone is united to one secular cause. It might feel like victory when a Christian is in political office. It might feel like winning when we hear things that make us feel like the Church is being empowered by our government. But it is loss. It is all loss. Because we have put our faith into something other than God when we rely on the government to make our lives better.

It is unparalleled hypocrisy to tell people that we are the example of Christ on earth, and then go to battle over a political candidate, destroying relationships, and making the Church inhospitable for anyone who disagrees with our choice. It is a hypocrisy that goes further than the personal kind that ignores the plank for the speck of sawdust (Matthew 7:3-5). It's the kind that damages the Church.

The first century church did not seek governmental power—they worked with what they had and became an example of what community could look like when it has something bigger to work toward, when its identity is Christ-centered and its goals are simply to live in God's vision for restoration.

When Jesus refused to rule under the restrictions that would have been in place with Satan's offer, He was choosing better for humanity.

We must do the same. We must choose better for our neighbors. We must set aside our pride in what we have built so they can see that human power structures will always fail. Only God deserves our allegiance.

TESTING GOD

In the final scene, Satan tempts Jesus by placing Him at the temple—the symbol of God's presence on earth—and tells Him to test God by requiring God to save Him in a visible, miraculous way. Jesus points out that the Scriptures tell us not to test God, and this section of the chapter ends with the Devil departing.

When Satan tried to convince Jesus that He should do this, that He should give people what they want—a God who leaves no doubt, one who works miracles for spectacle—Satan does so by misusing Scripture. Satan takes the verse about commanding angels out of the original context and uses it for his purposes. It's a warning about how easy it can be to take Scripture out of context to use for our agenda. Wielding the Word of God is an awesome responsibility.

At this point in the account, though, we see Jesus refuse the temptation and set aside the need to rule, the need to be recognized, and again the need to be the king that people expect, instead choosing to be the King that we need.

A King who does not succumb to the pressures that we place on Him to be anything other than an expression of God's love. A King that, like a good father, chooses what is best for us rather than giving us what we want.

When we, as individuals in the Church, take our experiences and plow through situations that we do not agree with, crafting the Church into an instrument of our image, using Scripture to highlight the issues that we think are important, are we not succumbing to the temptation to set ourselves up as king of the Church?

When we perceive that the world wants answers, do we try to fill in the space ourselves, or do we go back to the beginning, to relationship, to where Jesus found us, and remember that the Holy Spirit has work to do, and we are to be the example of Christ?

We are to be the ones who listen, who pray, who stand up to the temptation to prove God's existence by human methods when it seems like that is what they want. Like children, we don't always know what to ask for. Neither do those who don't believe in God. Why would we ever trade in Jesus's example of humble authority for the poor facsimile created out of human efforts?

Only a few verses later in the chapter, Jesus is rejected

in His hometown of Nazareth. He had faced suffering and stood up to the Devil, and His own people would not listen to Him.

But even in the face of rejection, Jesus didn't allow the message to change. Jesus didn't go back and try to convince them. He didn't reprioritize because of the results from a focus group; He didn't come up with a snappy marketing campaign. He was simply Jesus. The Savior. The example who lived out the truth that the King we need is rarely the king we want.

THE KING WE NEED
IS RARELY THE KING WE WANT.

MATURITY

We know that spiritual maturity is a journey that should never end. It is one in which we learn to love God back unconditionally, accepting that we must love God for who God is rather than who we want God to be. As we mature, we wade into the waters of service and humility, all the while remembering that our only witness is the love we are able to show.

We love God by loving what God loves: the Church.

But the Church is sometimes hard to love. People are hard to love. You and I are hard to love. So we lean into the only thing we can do, we study and pray and do our best to allow Christ's example to influence our every attitude. We set our priorities aside and listen to what the Holy Spirit tells us is important.

WE LOVE GOD BY LOVING WHAT GOD LOVES: THE CHURCH.

We love God back by creating an atmosphere where we can ask questions and where we do not always have to have a perfect answer. We love God back by realizing that when we are talking to each other, we are representatives of the Church, and as such we should not allow our own pet causes to draw the picture of the Church for another person. The Church is not our Church. It is God's Church.

We love God back by embracing each other, including our experiences as individuals.

We love God back by rejecting the temptation to appear successful, to hold the Church up to human standards, to try to convince the world that we are not different. Because we are. We are so different. We follow a law that requires power structures to melt away. We follow teachings that demand we give up anything that looks like worldly success. We are different. We should be different.

At the call of the Holy Spirit, we allow ourselves to fall in love. And falling in love changes us.

When we fall in love, we look foolish and we don't care.

When we fall in love, no sacrifice is too great. When we fall in love, we see the other person as God sees them, with all their potential intact and their past erased. When we fall in love with the people in our lives, we are living as Christ did, and we can't help but be the Church Jesus wants.

So we become unexpected revolutionaries. We don't carry banners, we don't fight for political wins, we don't try to shape the world into our image.

Instead, we live this life, constantly choosing to shape ourselves into the image of God.

SPECIAL THANKS

To my pastor friends, who worked diligently, and often at great personal cost, to make sure that the gospel they preached did not change under the pressures of the last few years.

To Pastors André Robinson and Zach Mueller for their friendship and for the countless hours spent in conversation, working through the ideas that eventually became this book.

To Pastor Laurie Tenpenny for encouraging me to write it.

To Pastor Lisa Larson and the rest of our sermon writing group for being my sounding board.

To my parents, Pastor Tom and Linda Edwards for being my first readers and advocates.

And to my husband, David Luecht, because without your support and love, this book would have been impossible to write.

Printed in Great Britain
by Amazon

12395938R00119